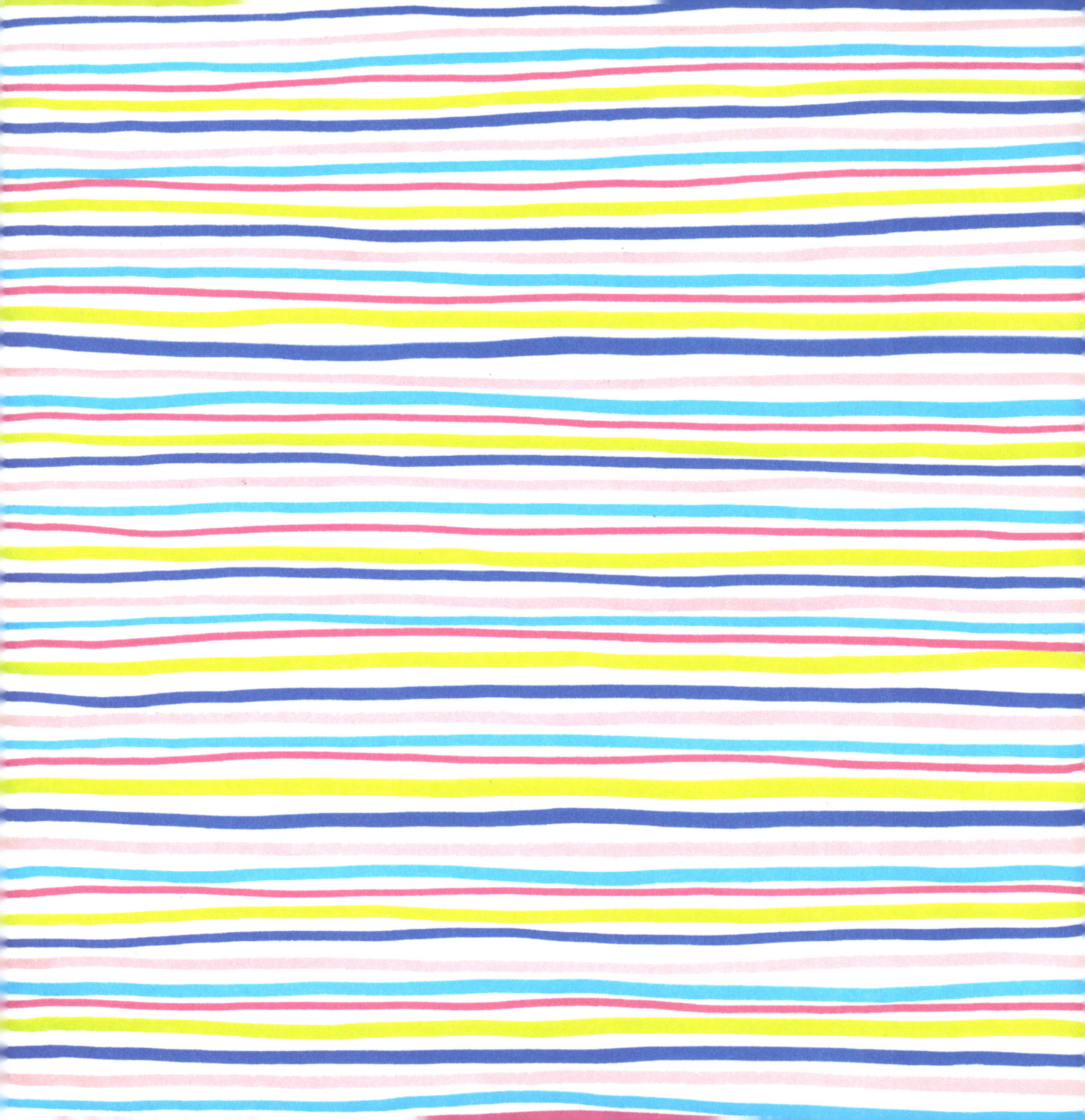

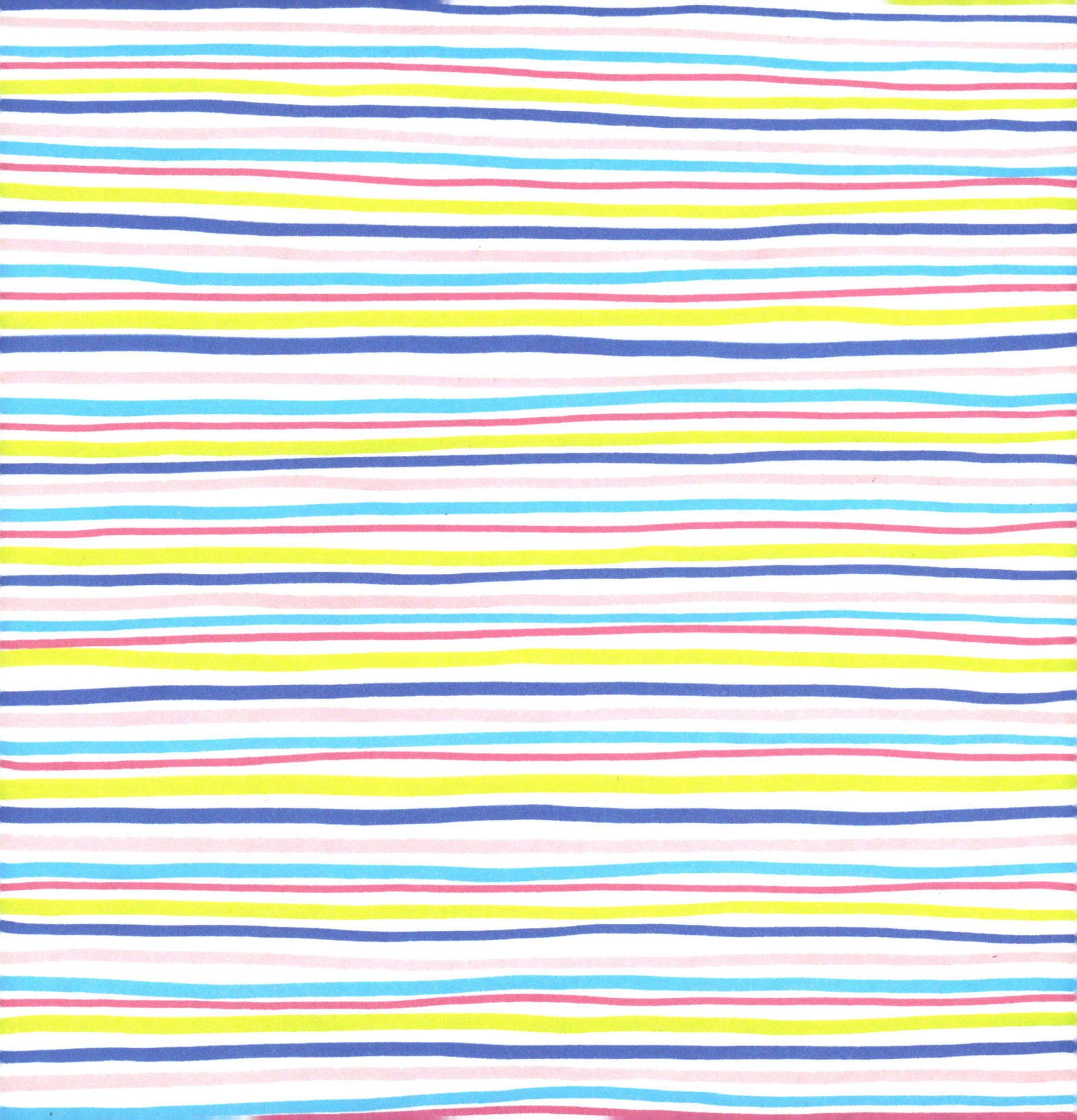

Books may be purchased in quantity or special sales by contacting the author at IFeelWeirdBook@gmail.com.

Published by: Wish on Everything and CreateSpace
This book was made possible by a Kickstarter campaign in Spring 2013.

ISBN: 978-0-991158-00-3

First Edition

For more information and to contact the author, visit: http://www.georgiakoch.com.

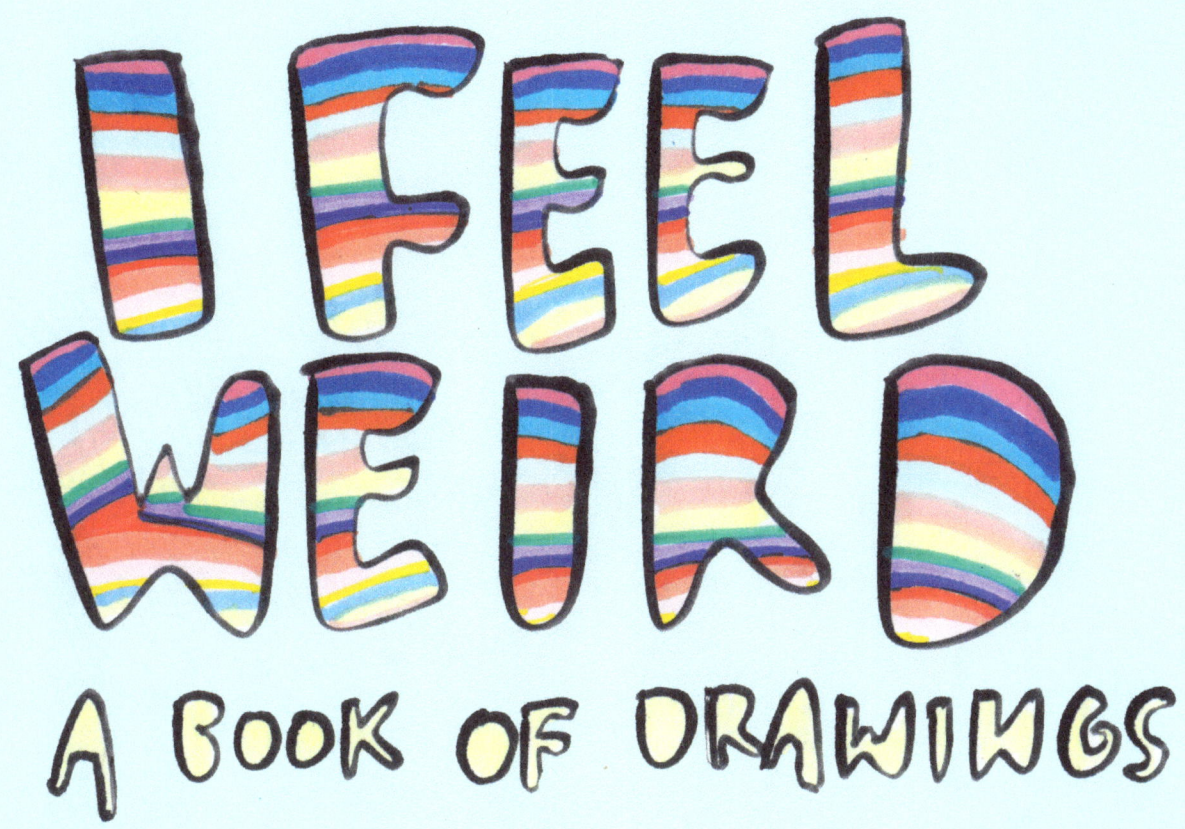

I FEEL WEIRD

A BOOK OF DRAWINGS

BY GEORGIA KOCH

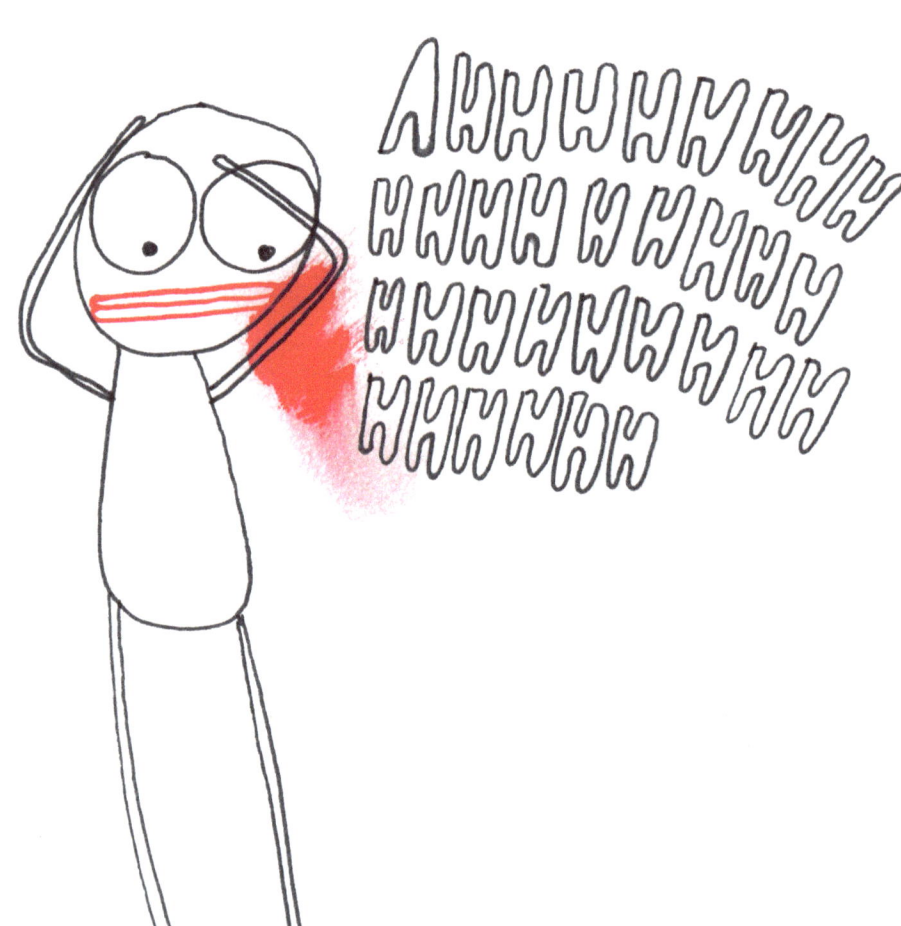

STOP JUDGING ME.

ABOUT THE AUTHOR

AGE 24
FEMALE
LOS ANGELES, CA

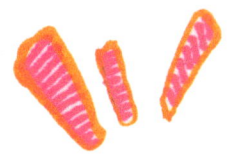

THIS BOOK WAS MADE POSSIBLE BY KICKSTARTER AND THE 136 PEOPLE THAT BACKED MY CAMPAIGN.

THANK YOU.

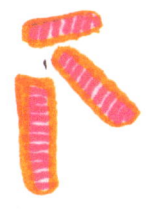

YOU DONT ACTUALLY HAVE TO READ THIS BOOK.

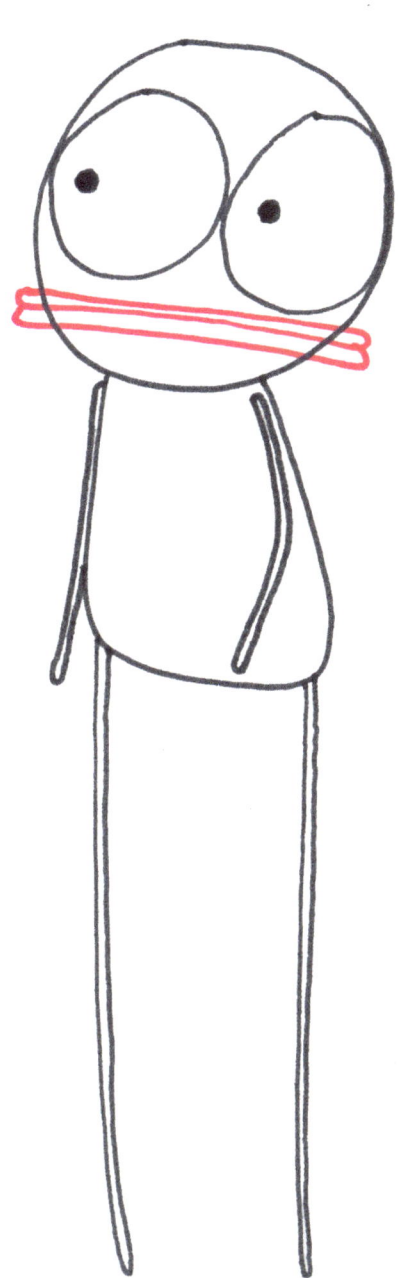

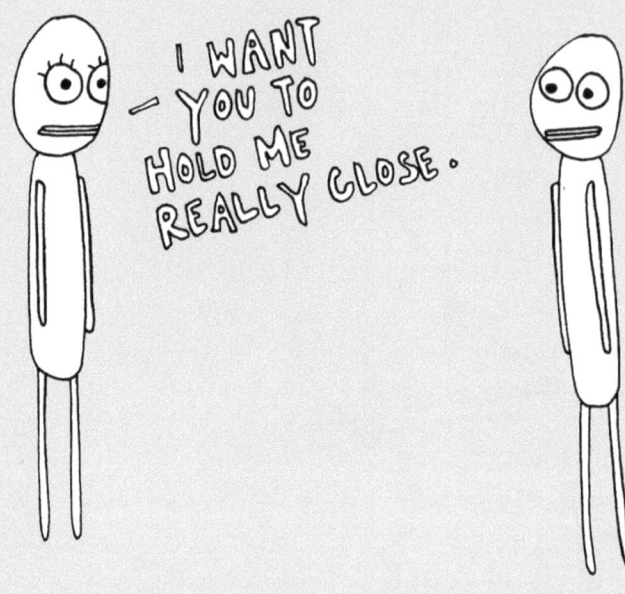

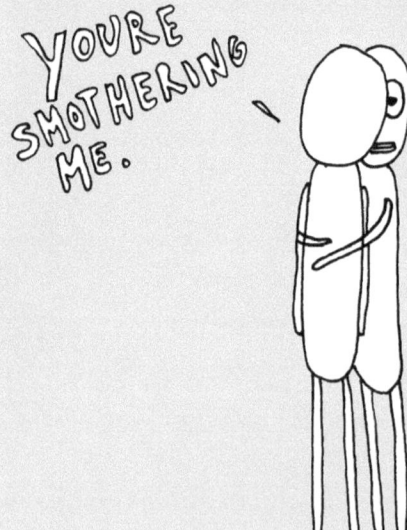

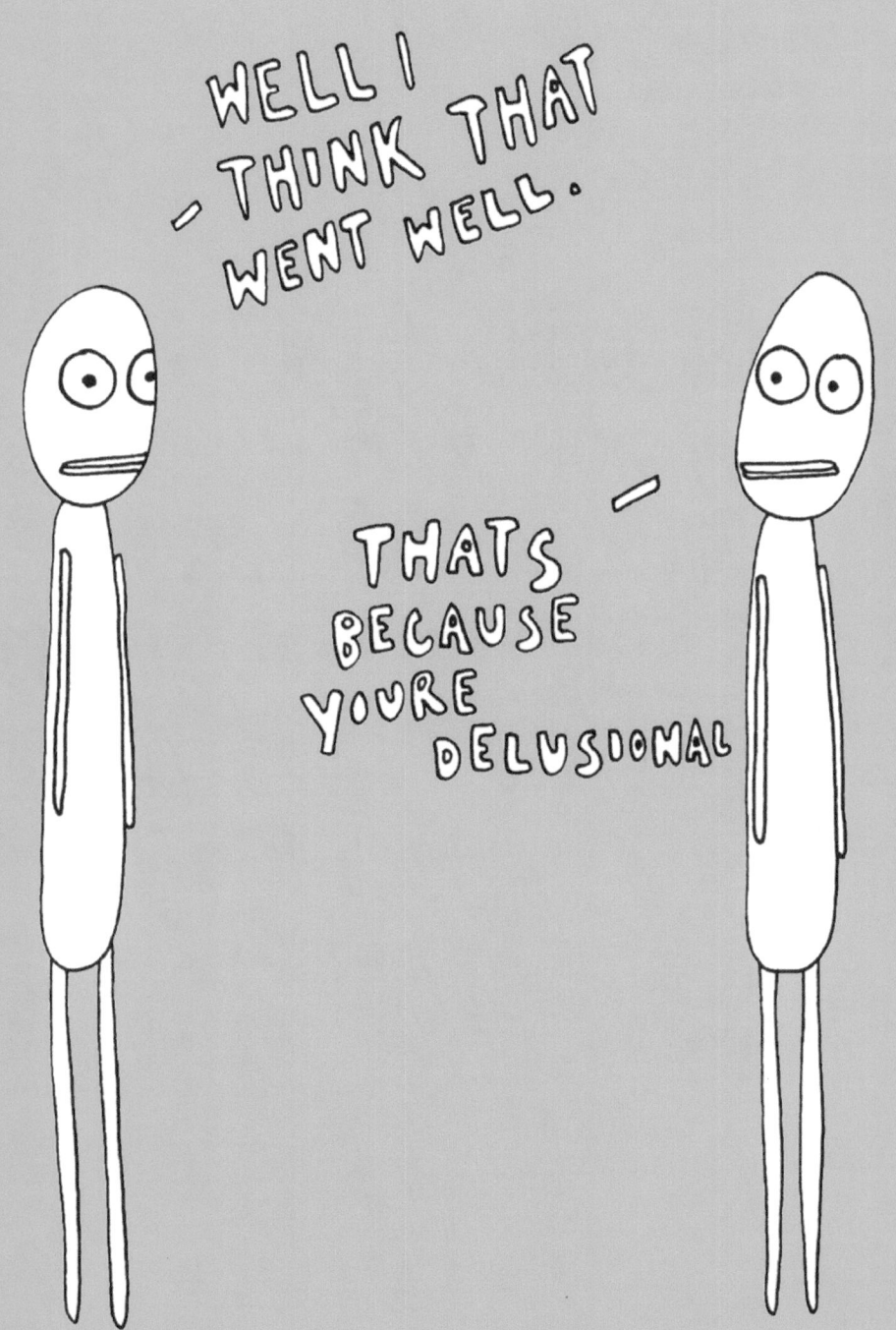

I MIGHT LOOK WEIRD, DIFFERENT, OR NOT INTERESTING ENOUGH. I MIGHT NOT BE AS GOOD AS SHE IS - BUT I AM ME... AND I DO CARE A WHOLE LOT ABOUT EVERY-THING. ESPECIALLY YOU.

PART ONE
EVERYBODY
SUCKS.

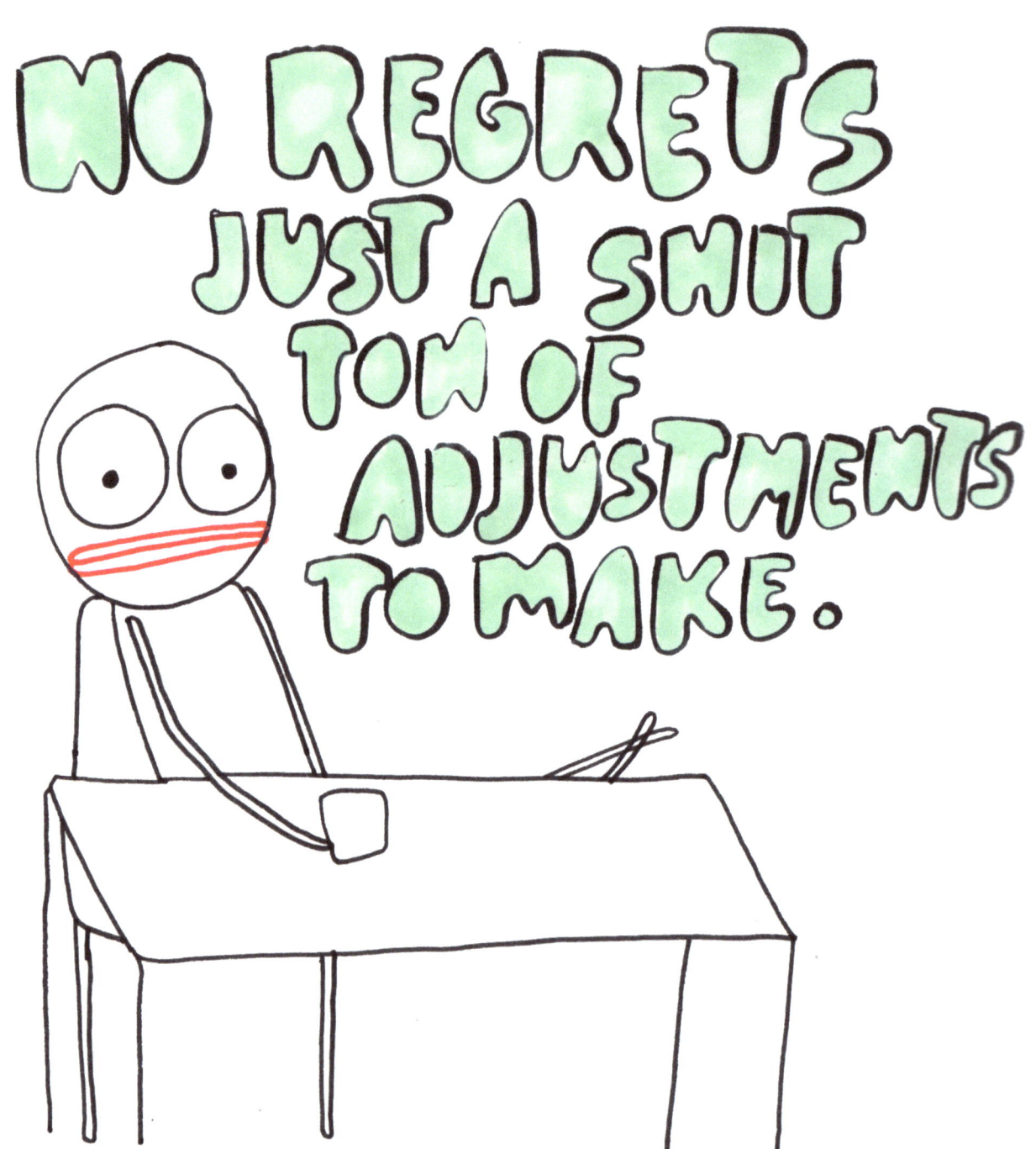

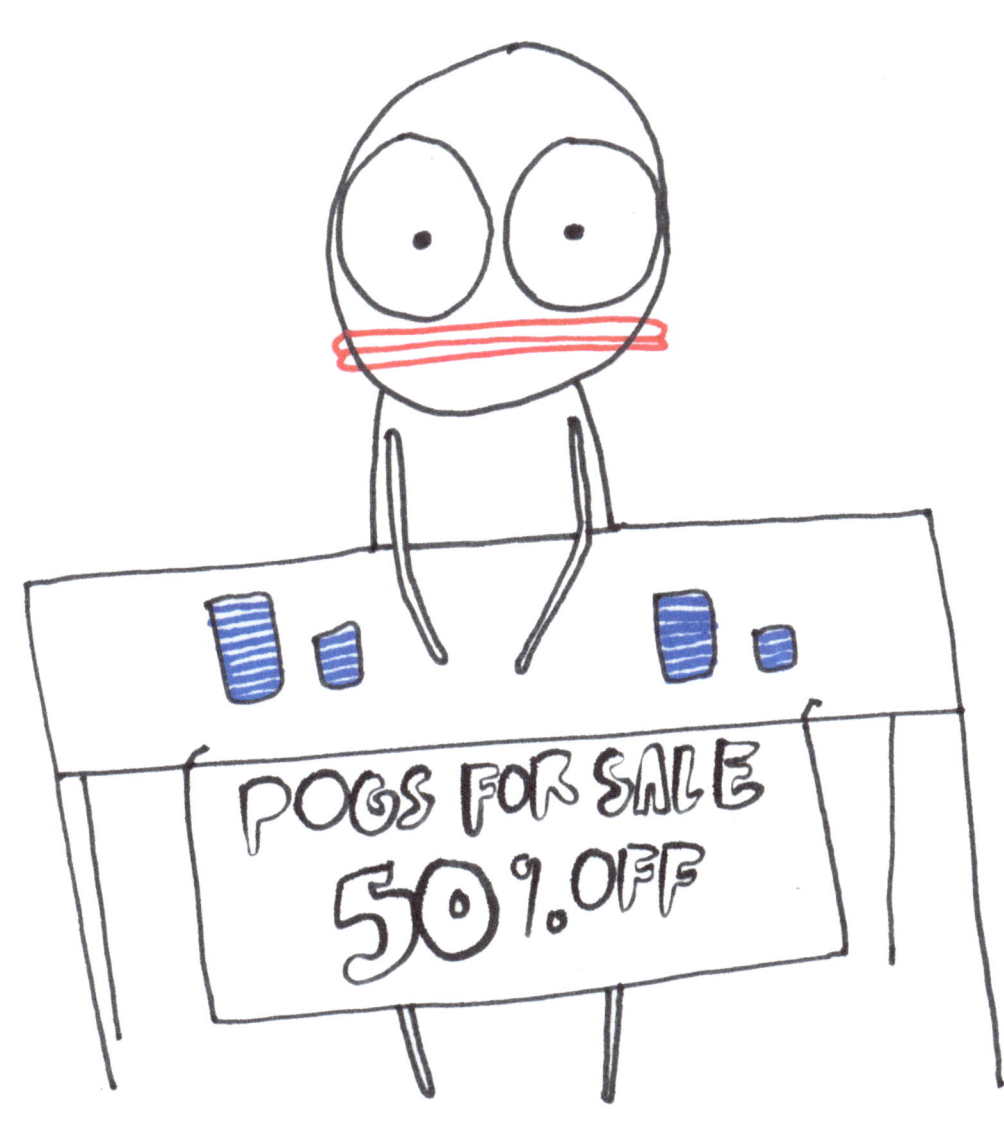

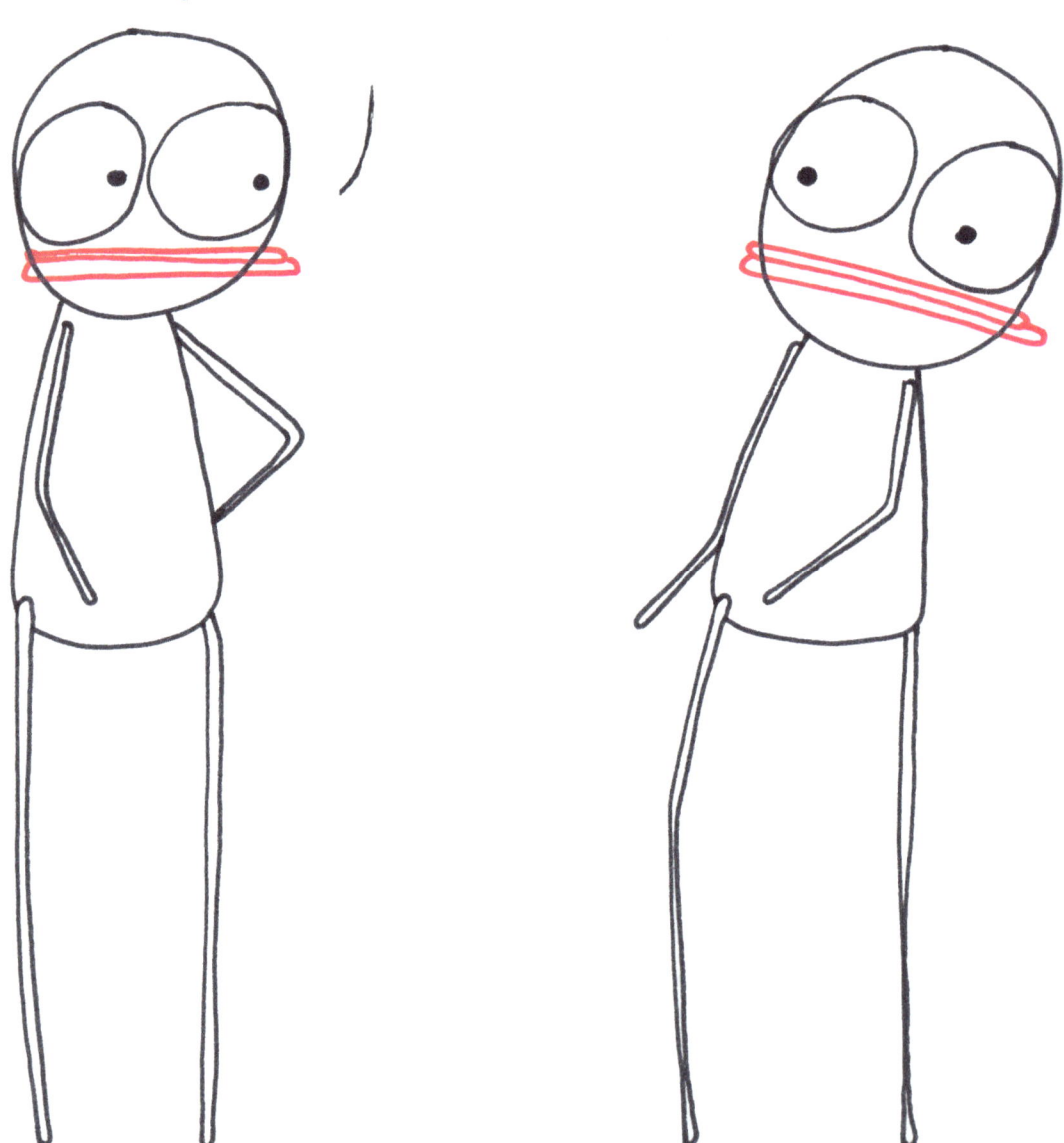

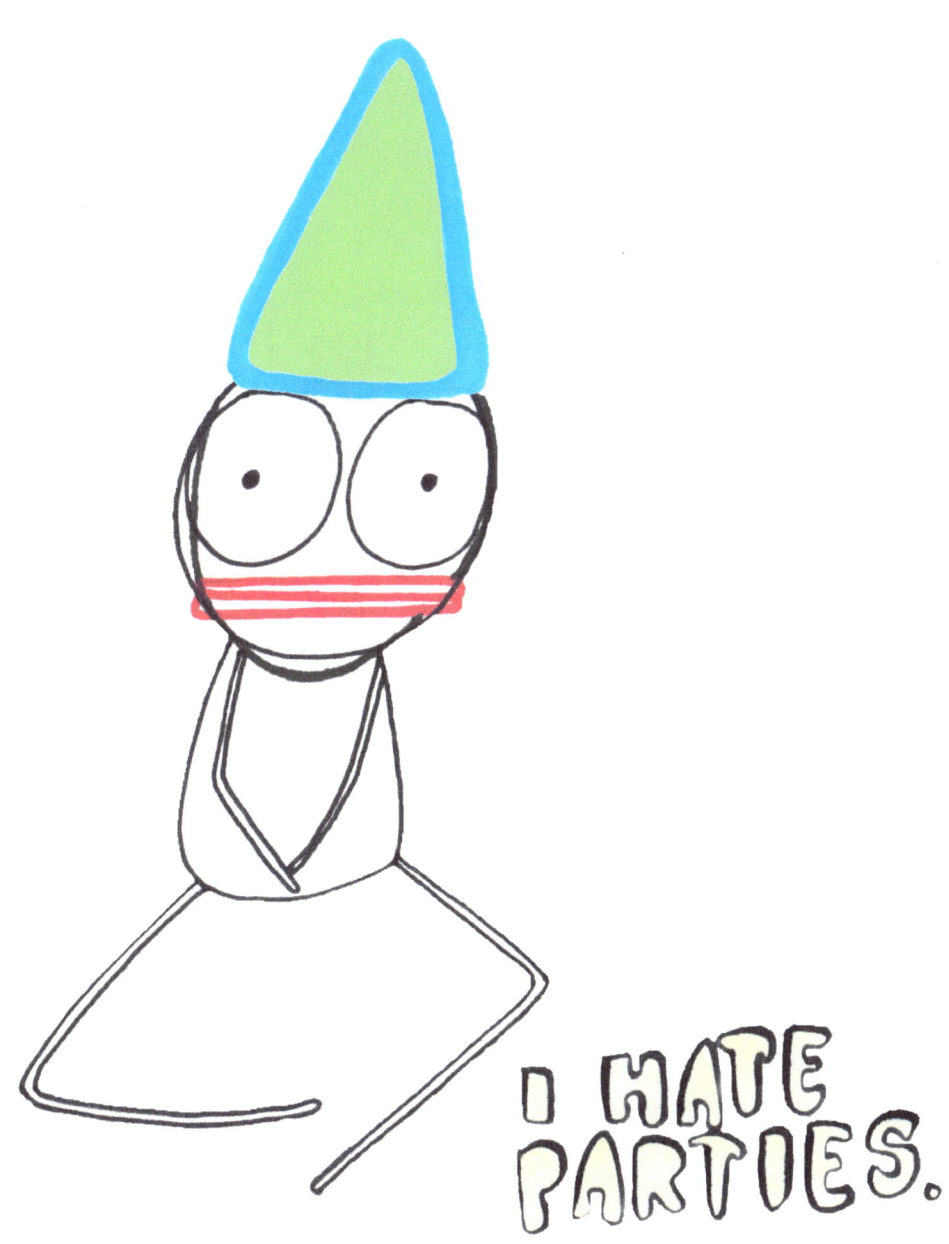

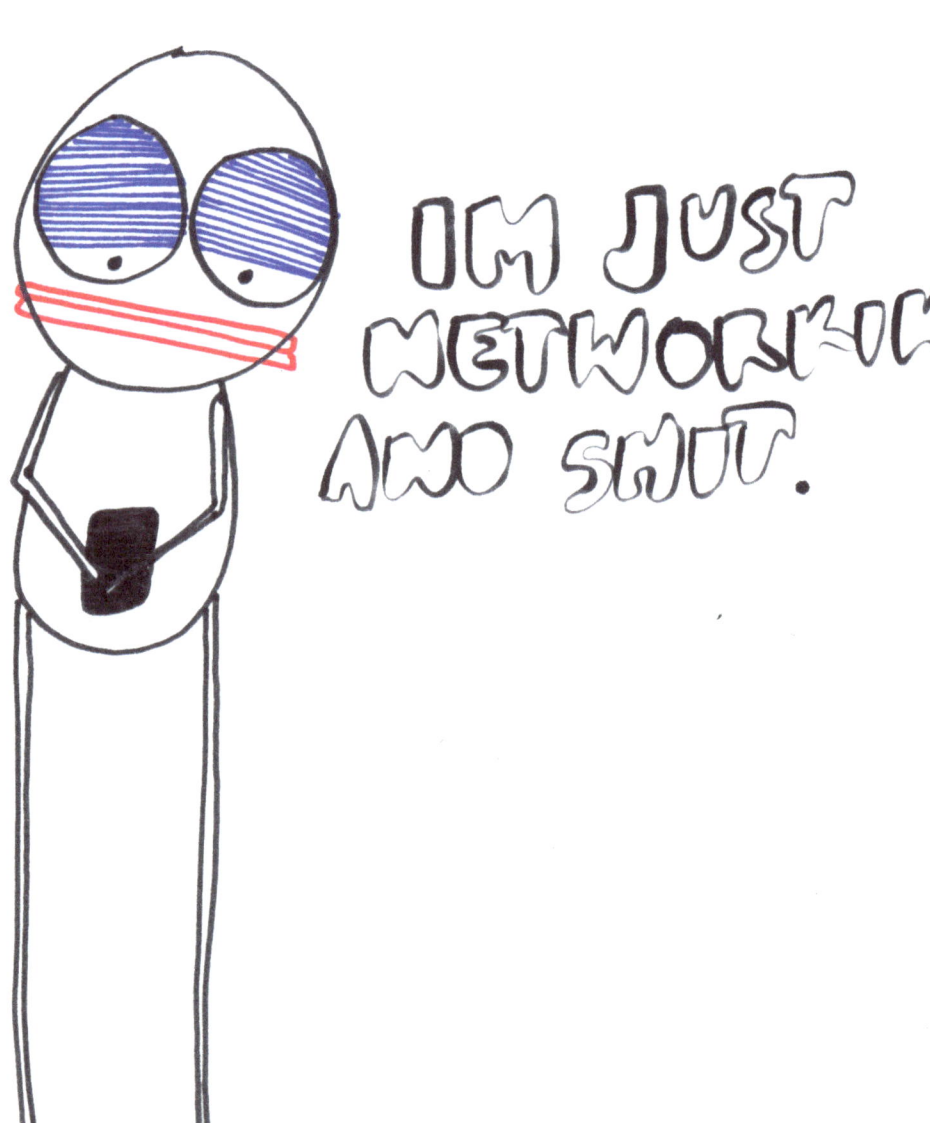

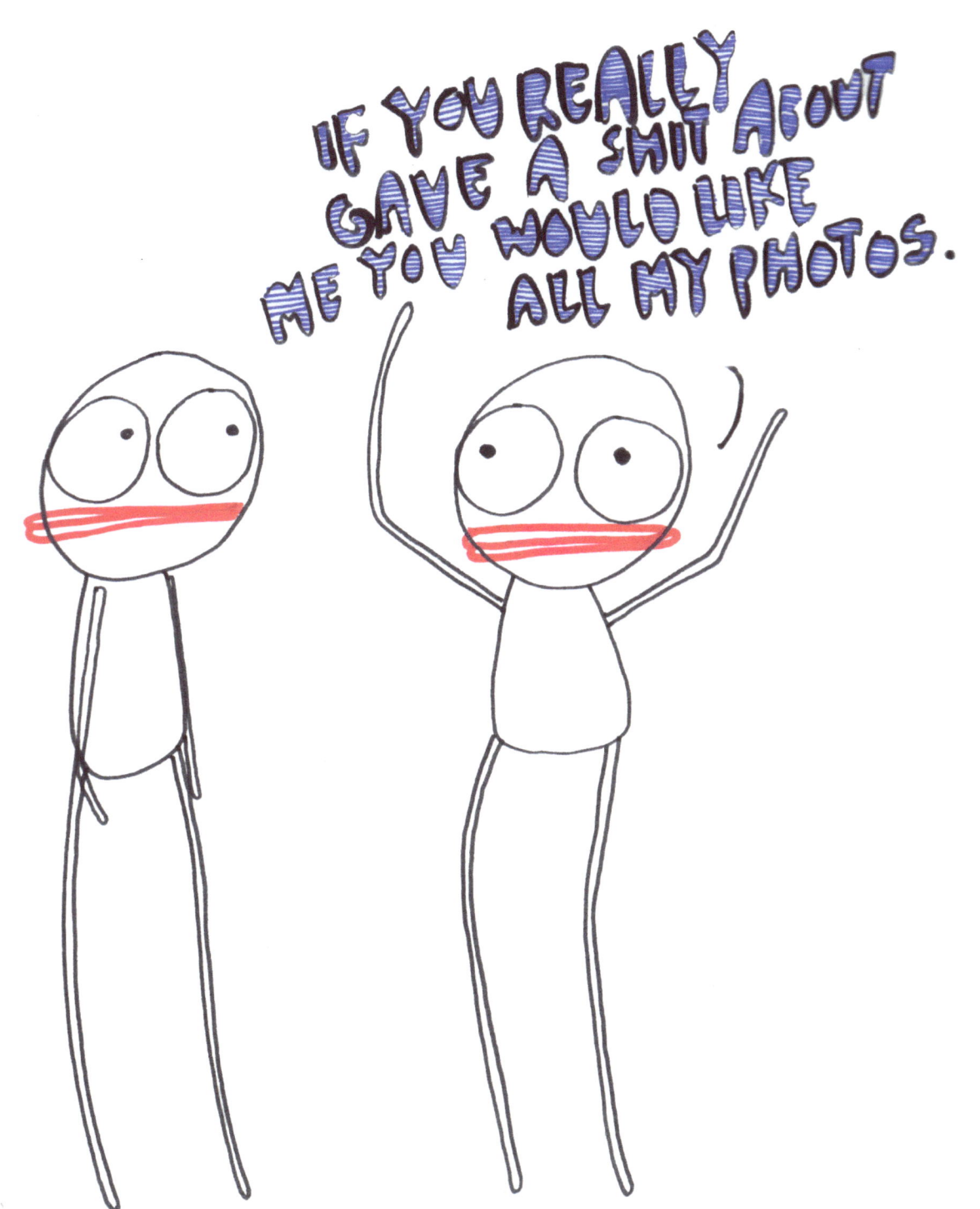

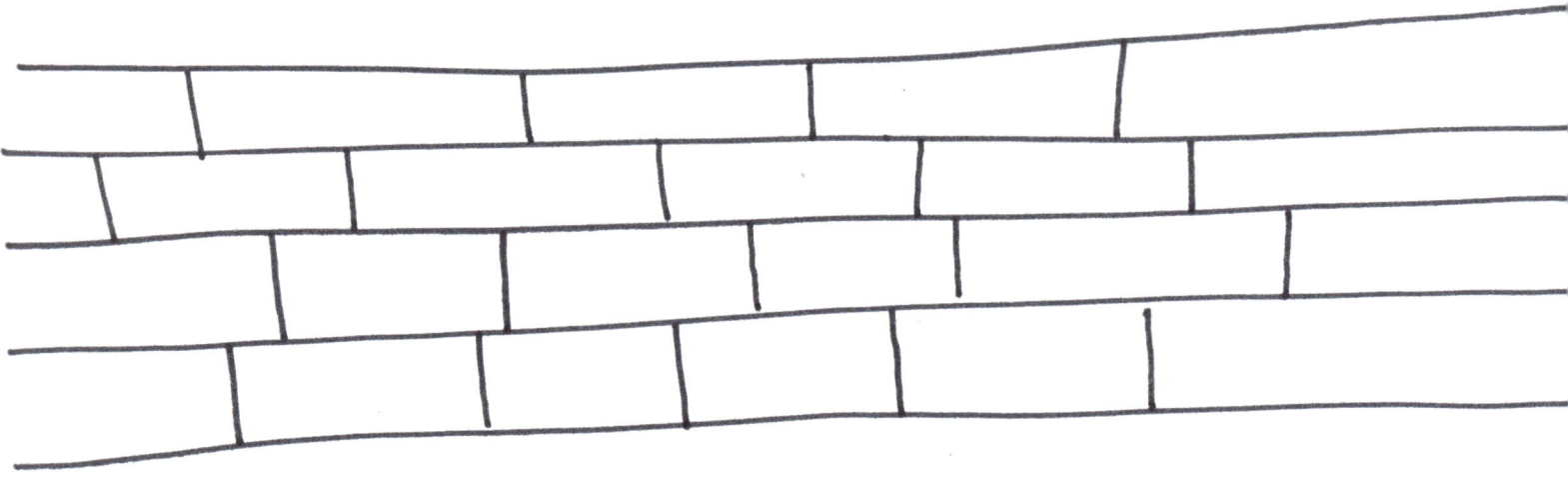

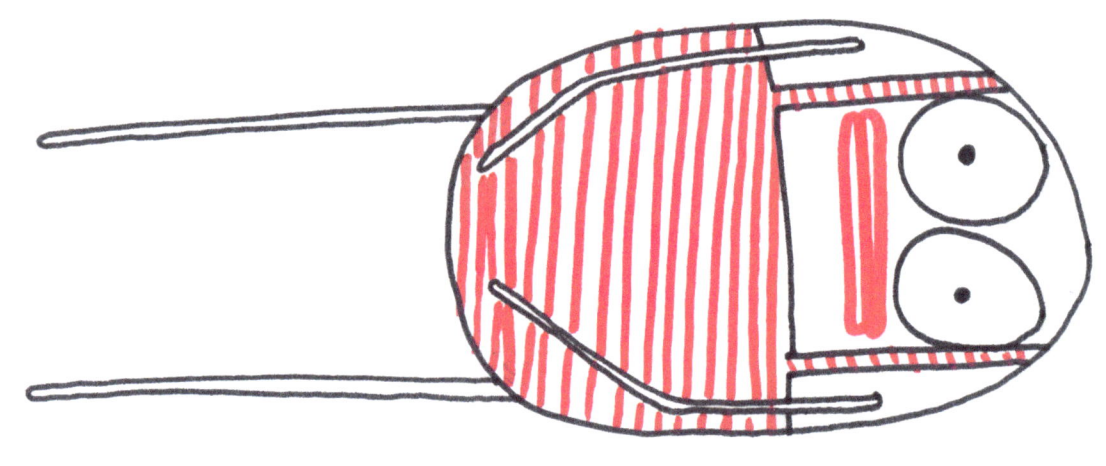

HUMPTY DIED & NOBODY CARES.

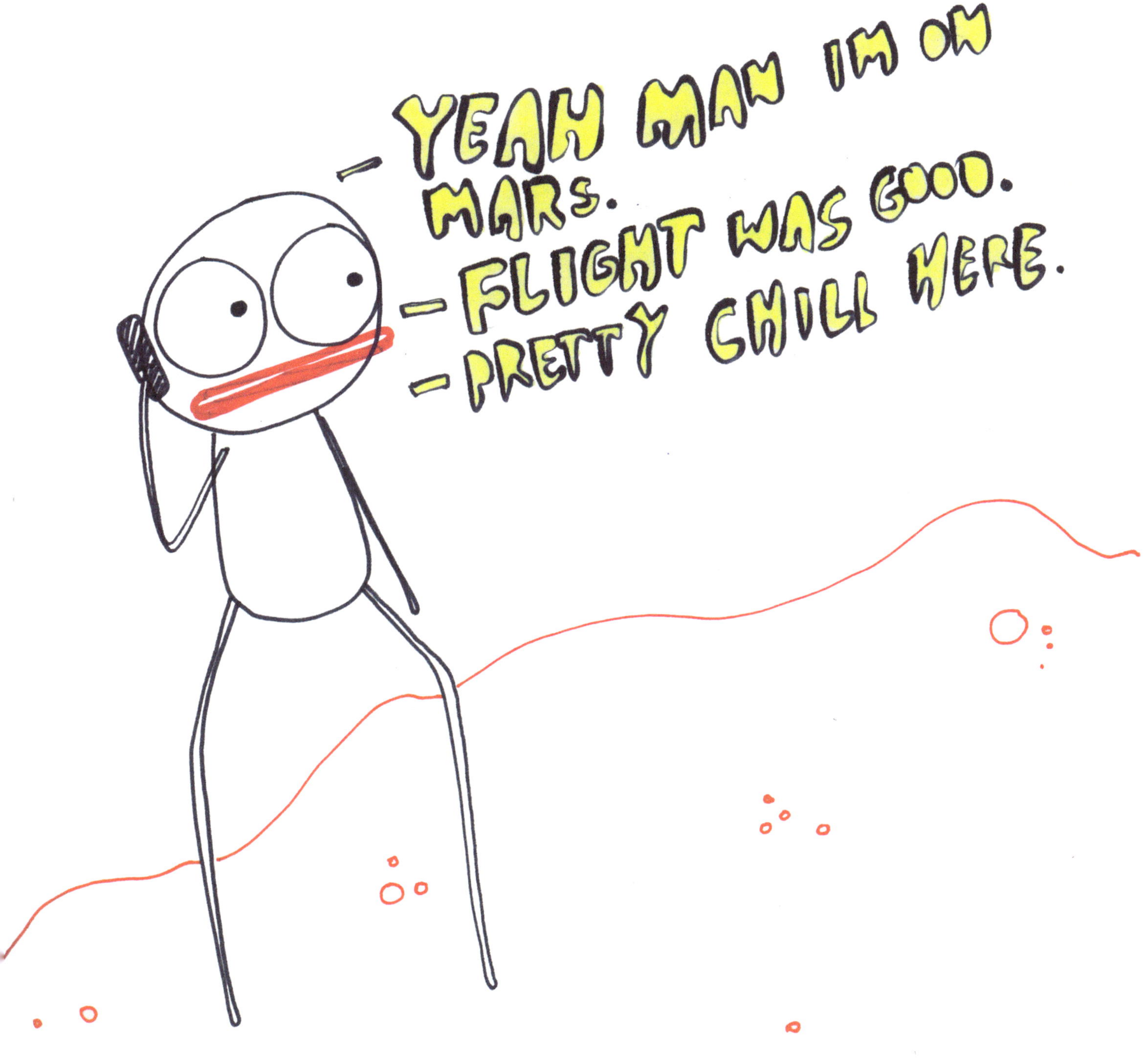
-YEAH MAN IM ON MARS.
-FLIGHT WAS GOOD.
-PRETTY CHILL HERE.

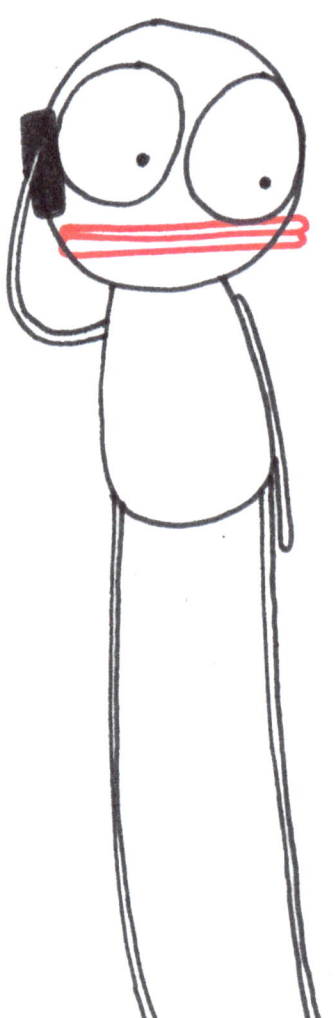

SIRI DO YOU LOVE ME?

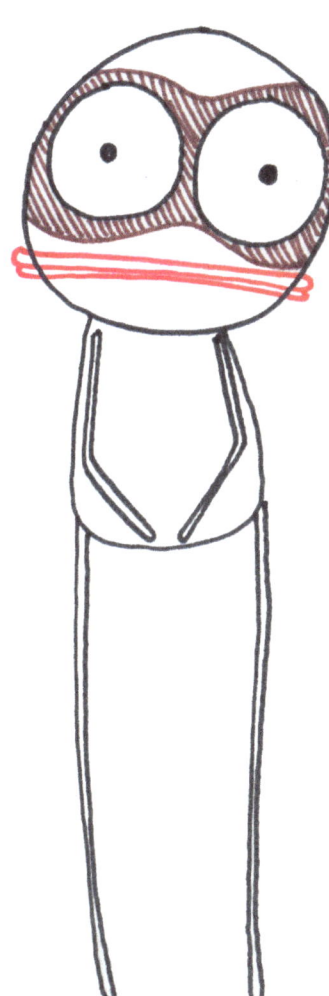

REAL NINJAS NEVER TELL.

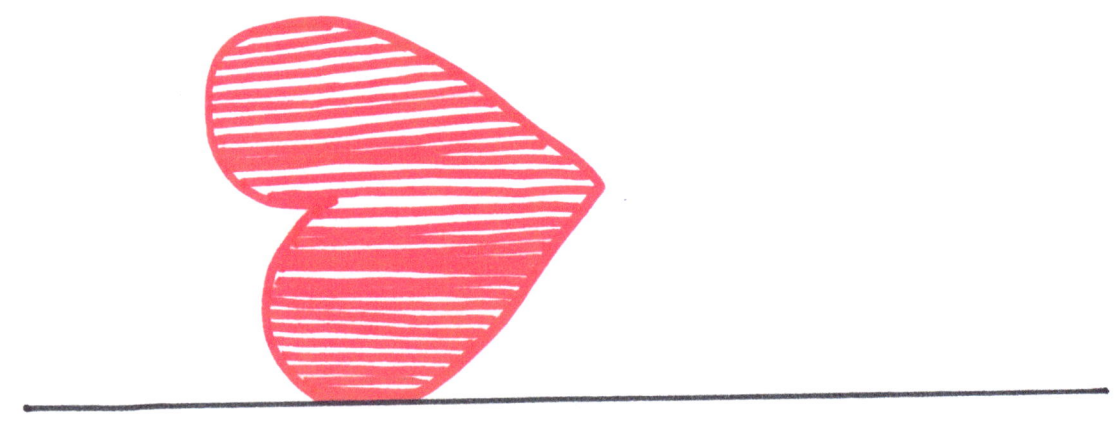

PUT YOUR HEART ON THE LINE.
(SEE EXAMPLE ABOVE.)

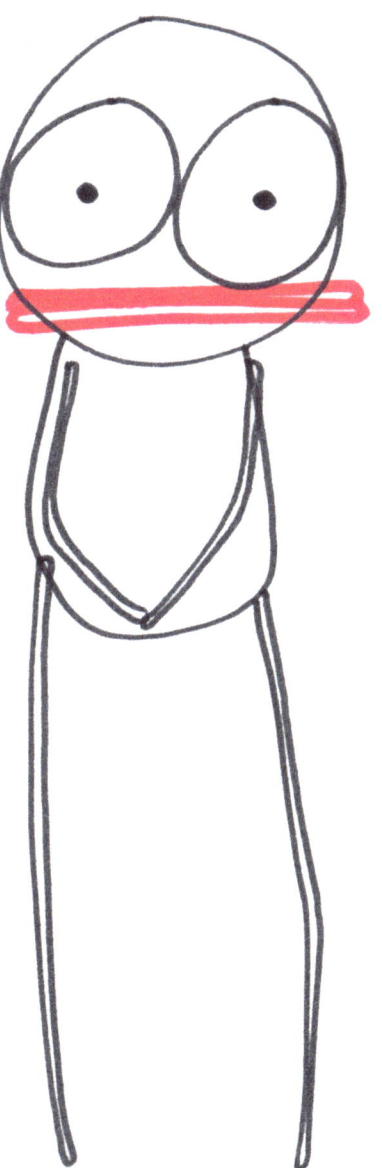

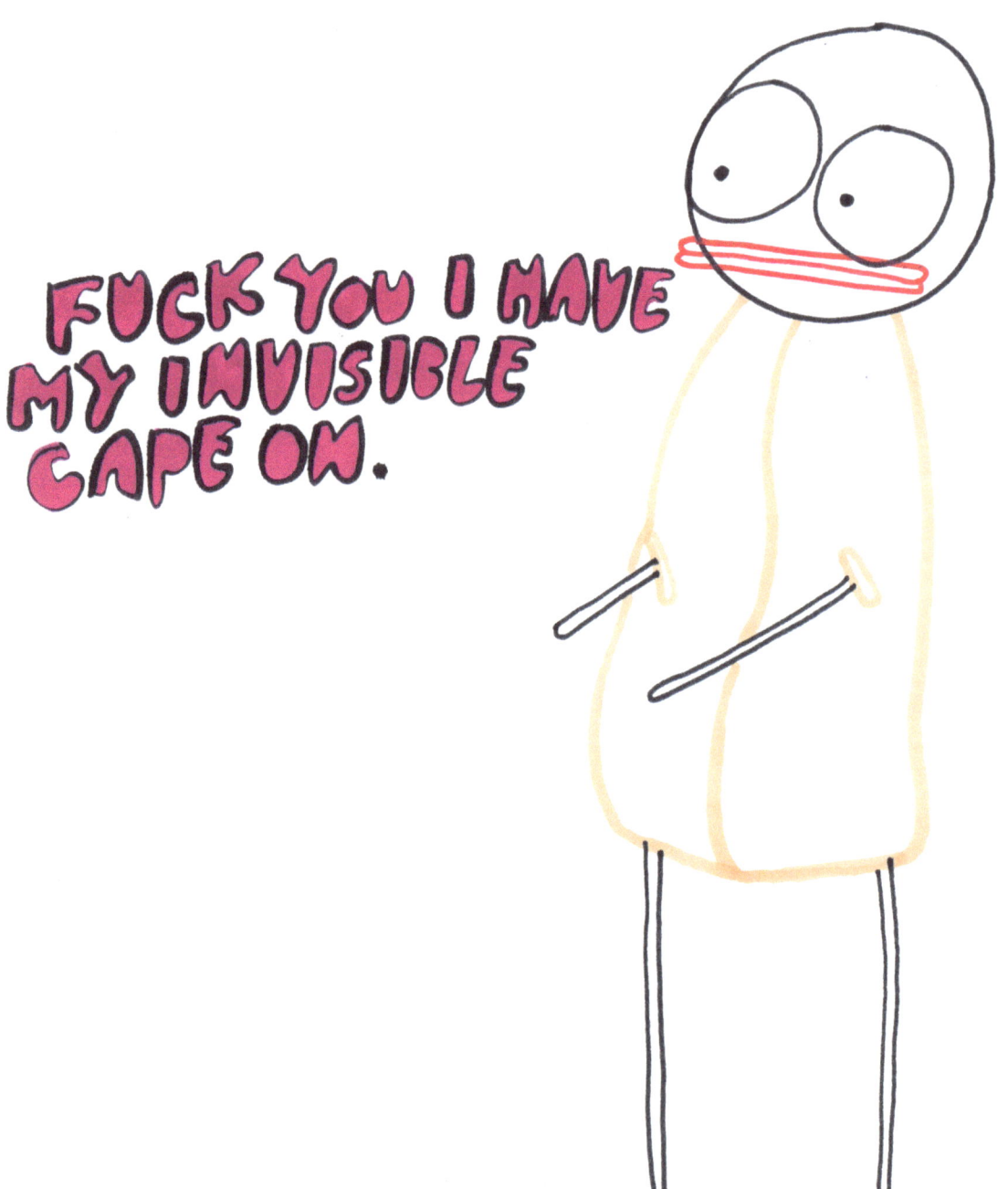

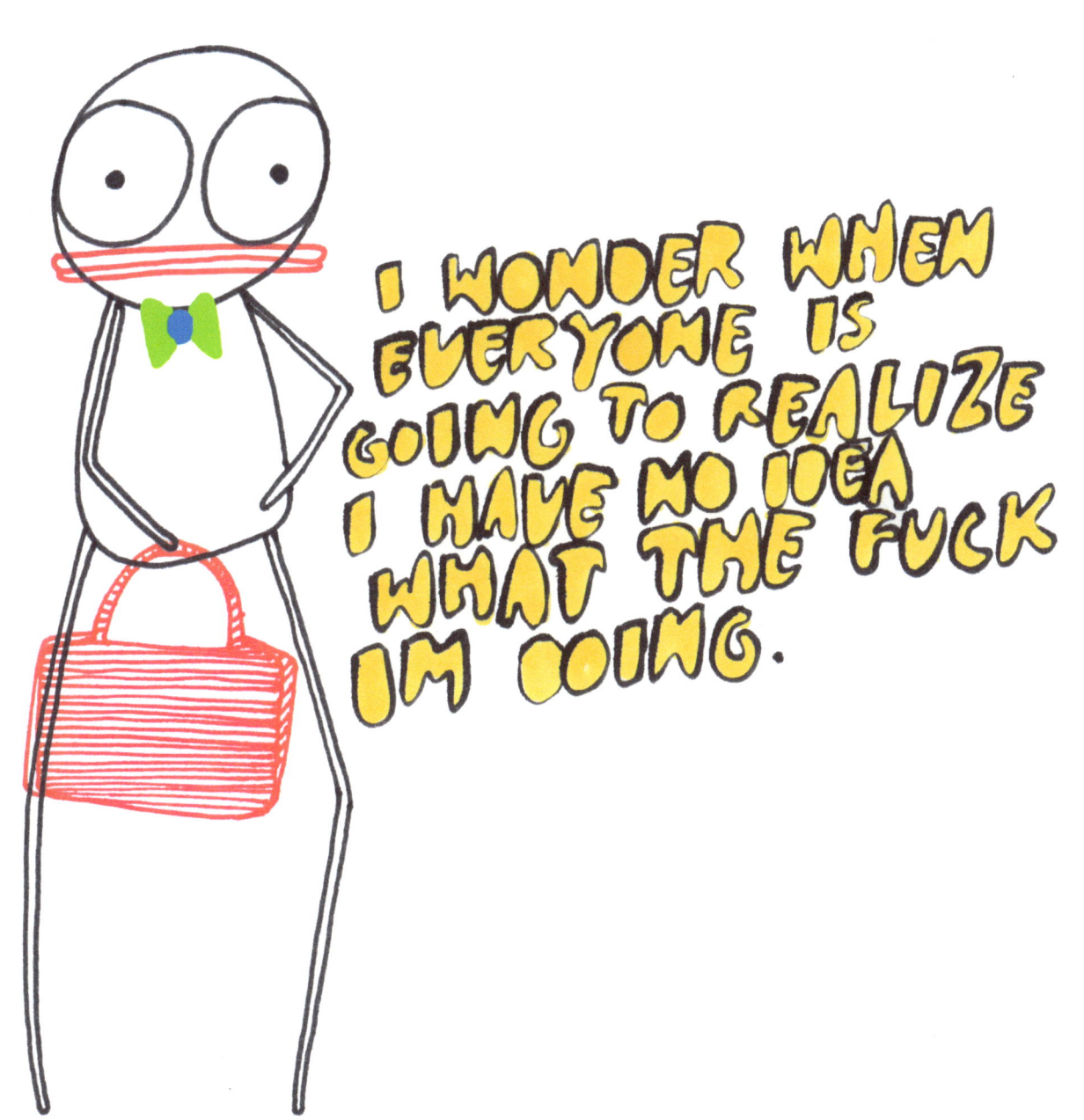

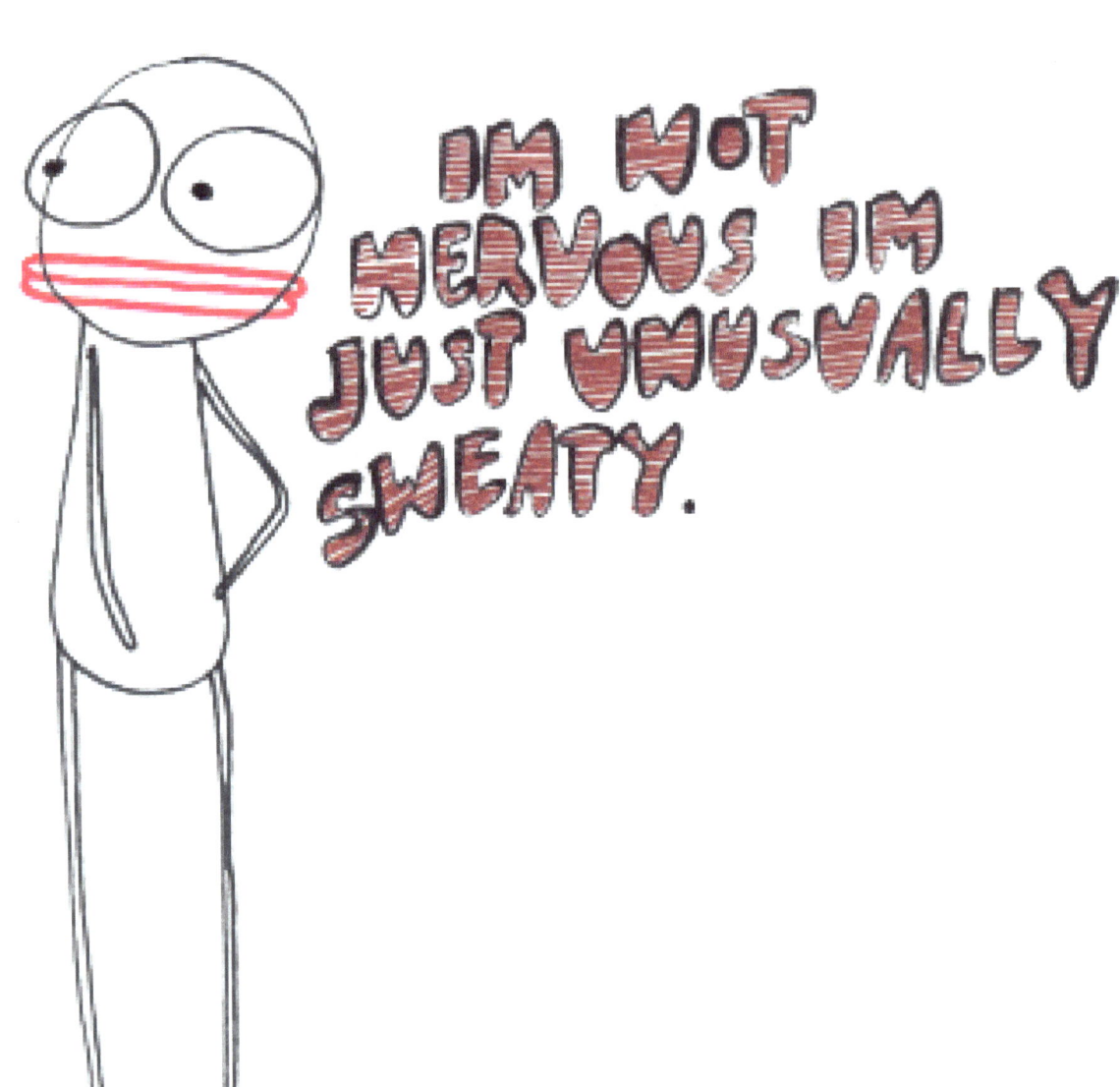

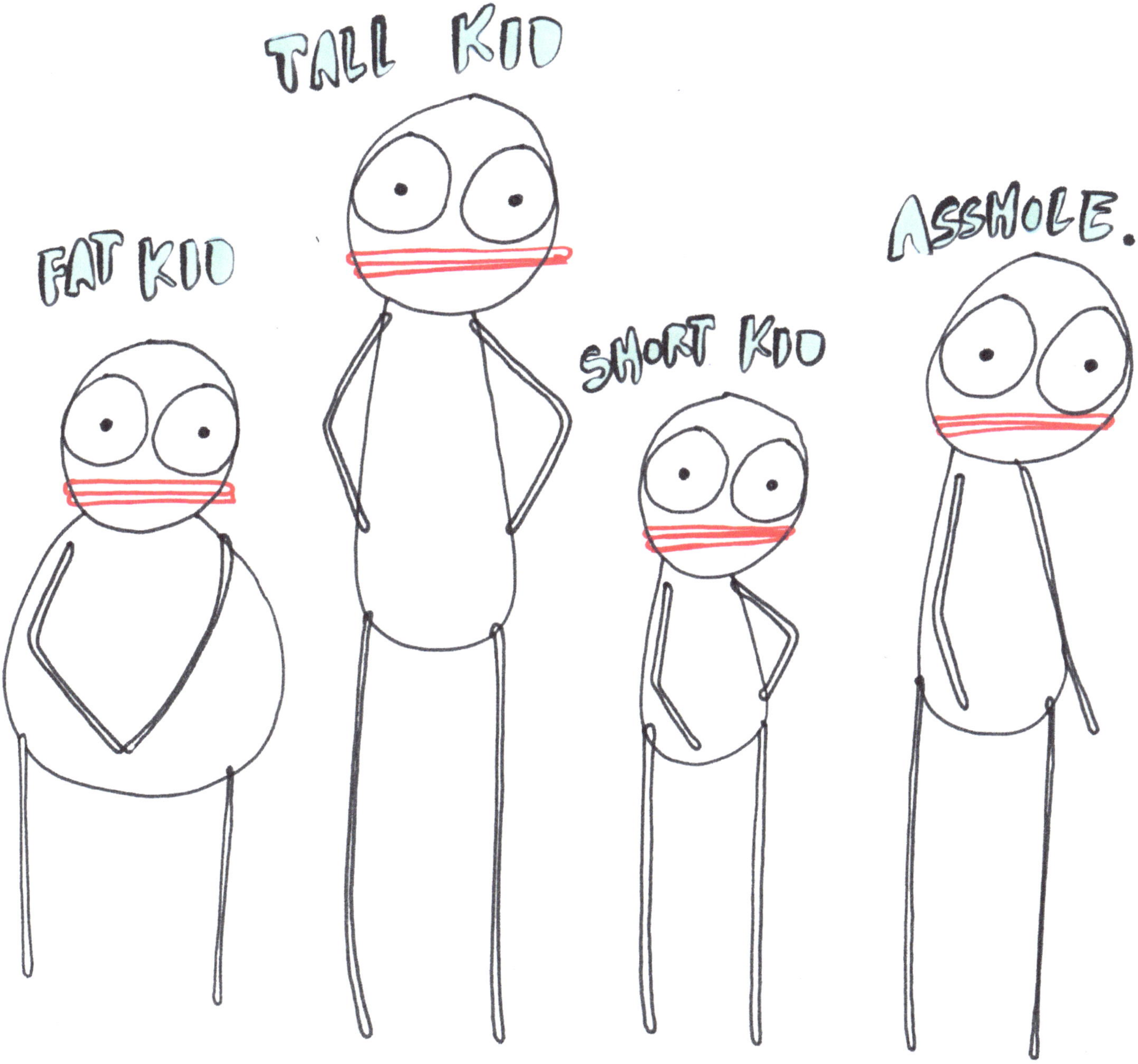
FAT KID
TALL KID
SHORT KID
ASSHOLE.

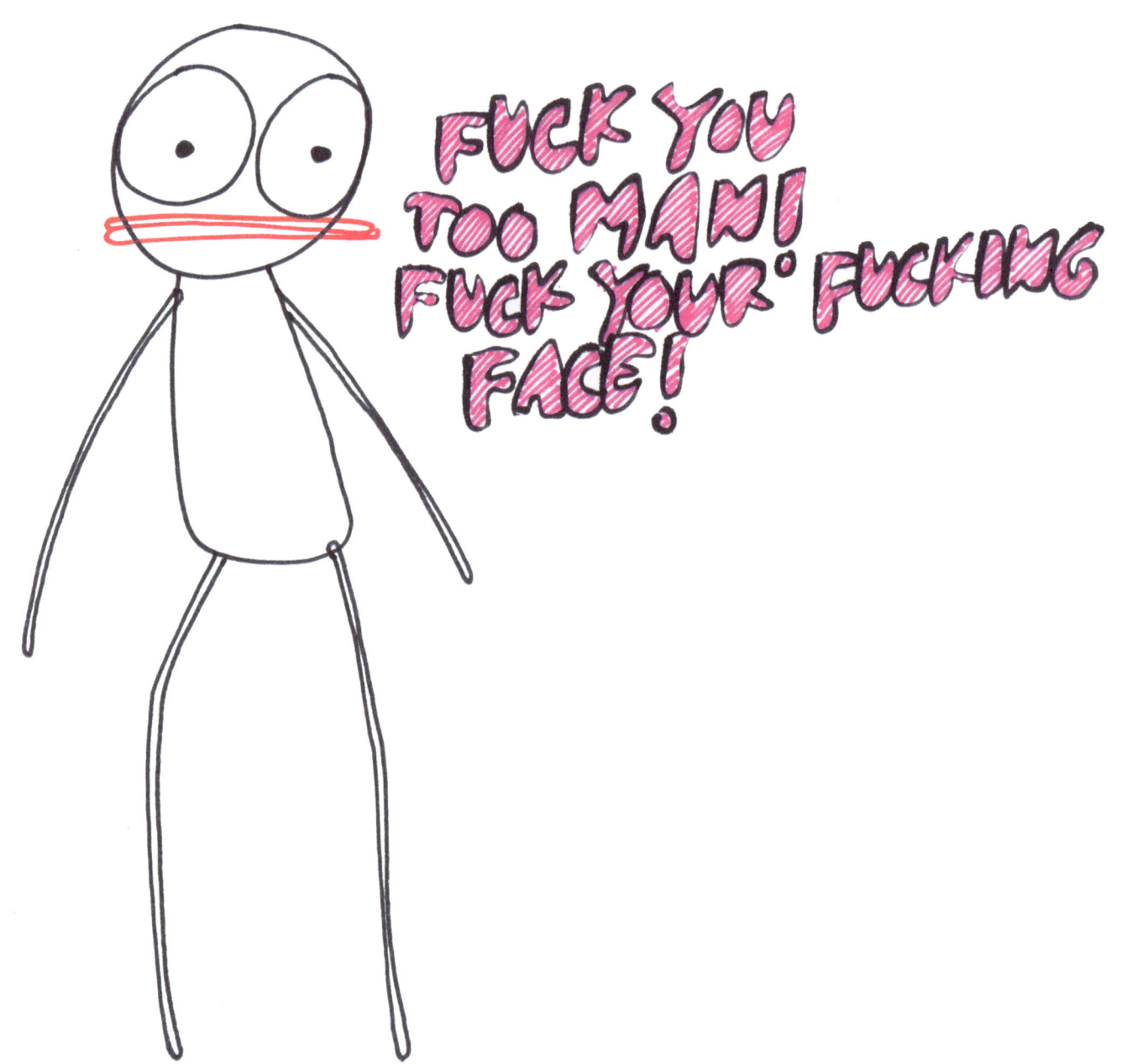

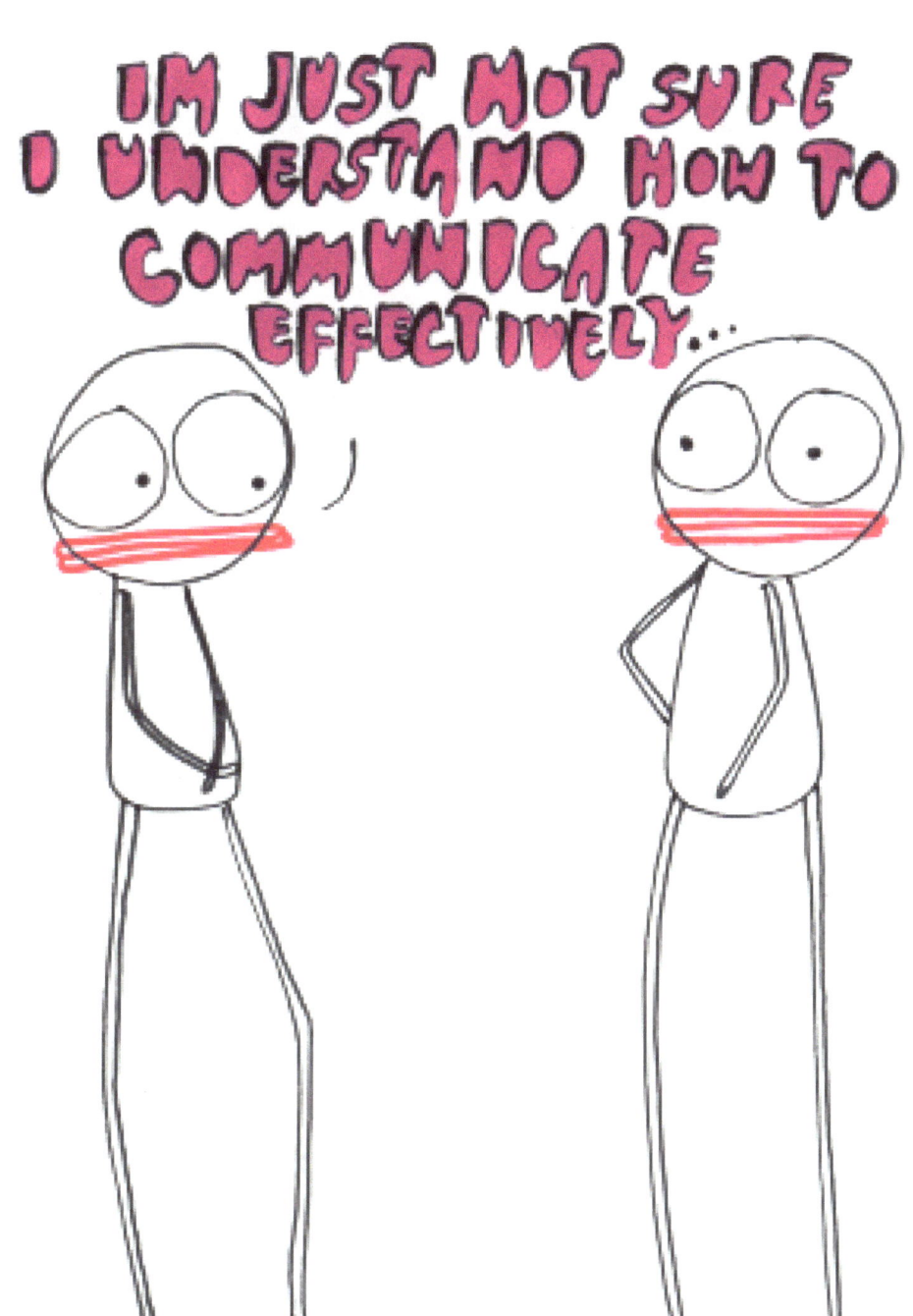

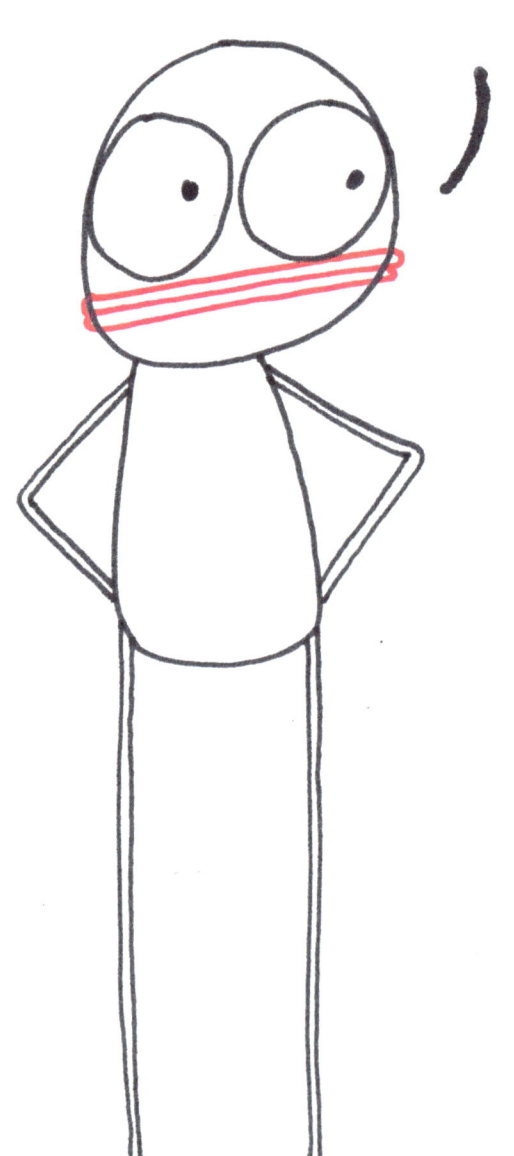
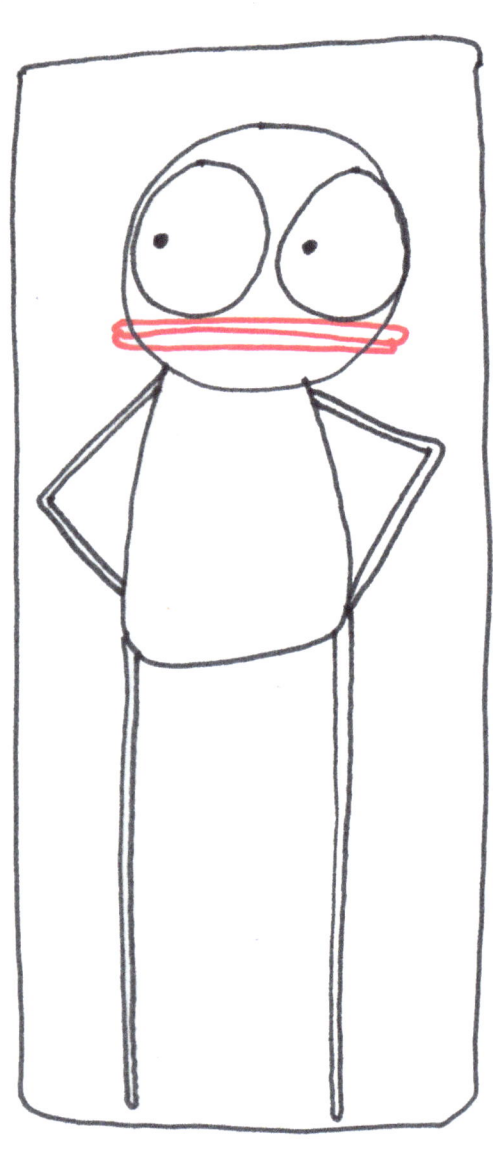

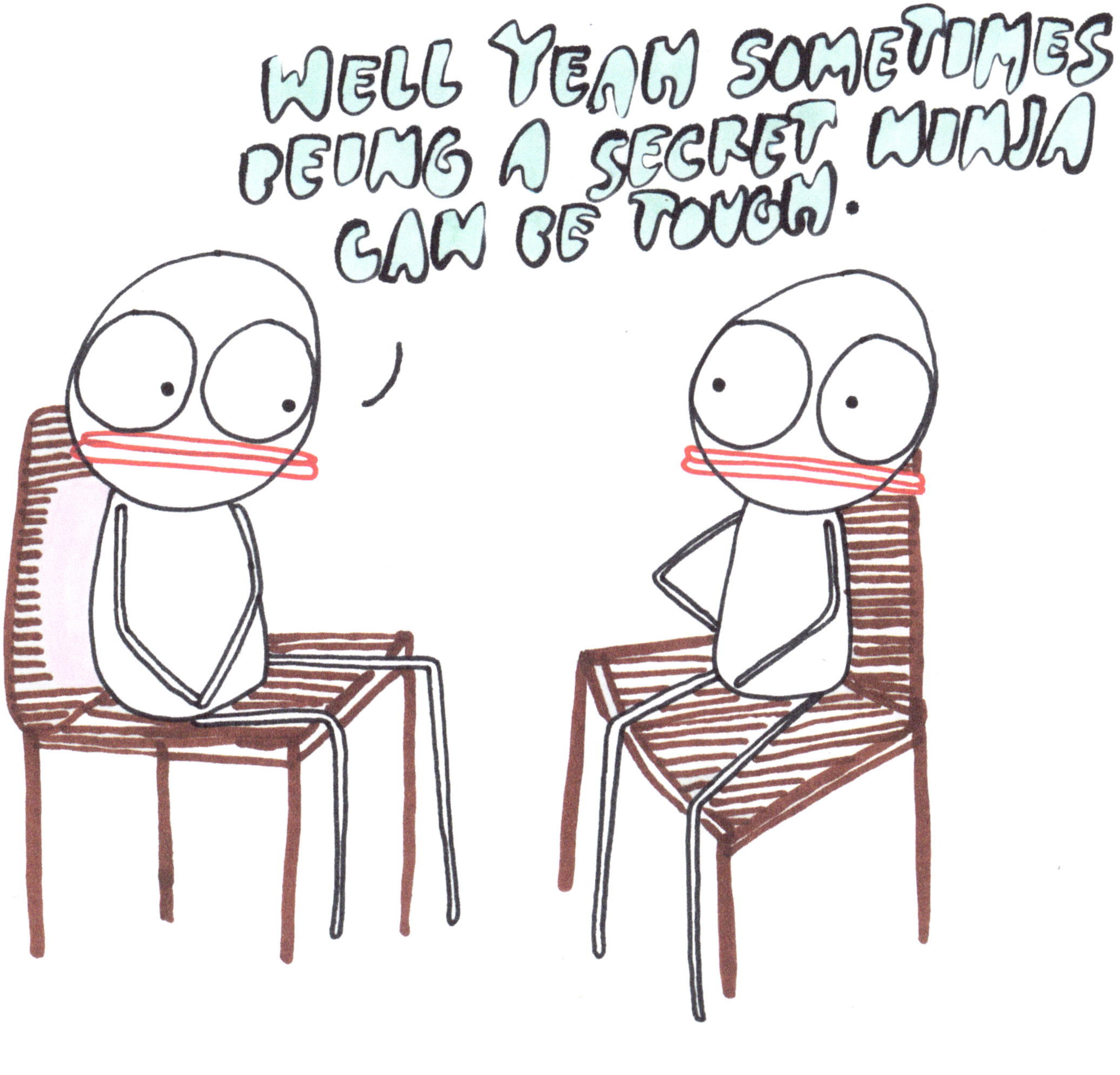
WELL YEAH SOMETIMES BEING A SECRET NINJA CAN BE TOUGH.

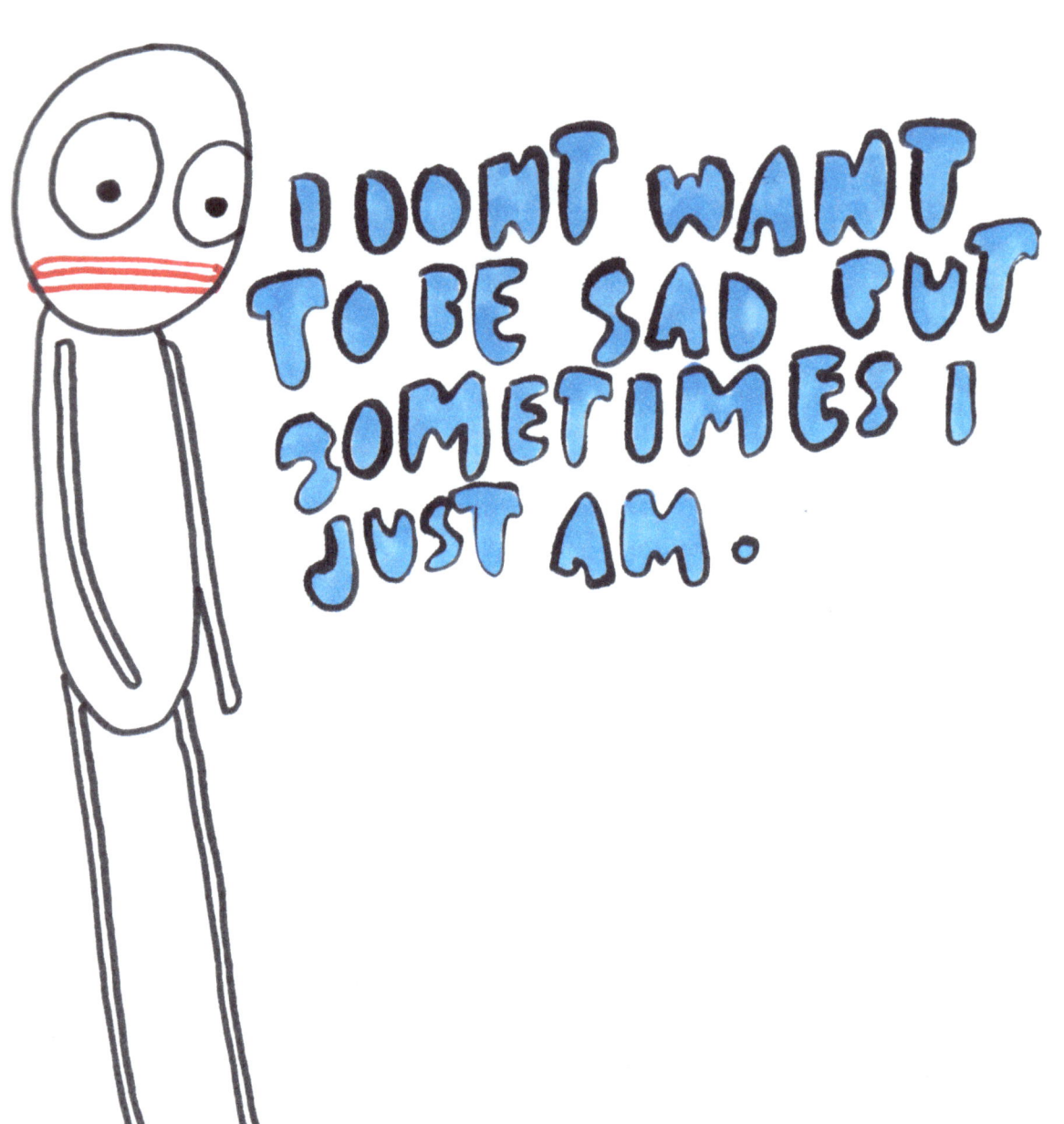

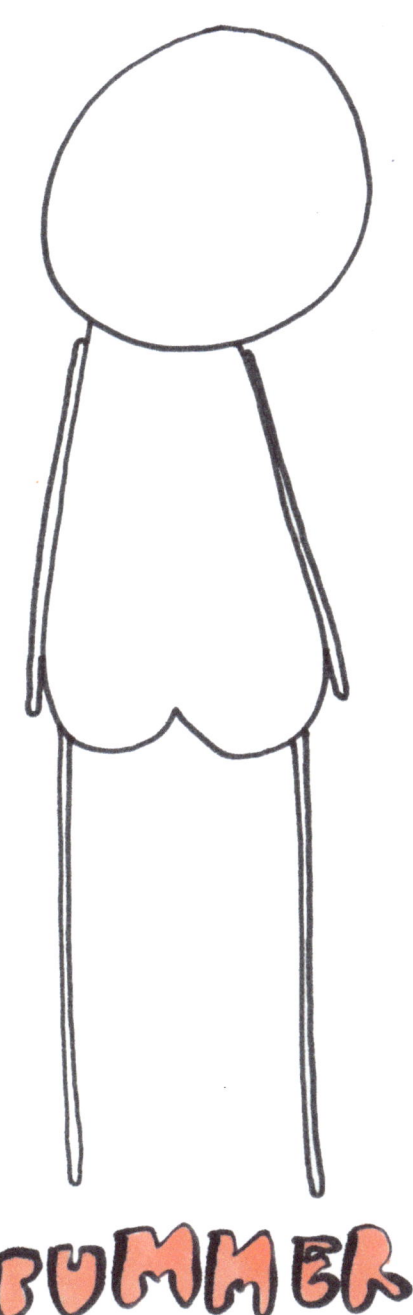

BUMMER.

I'M NOT THE CLASSIC PROFILE OF WHAT THE LADIES WANT.

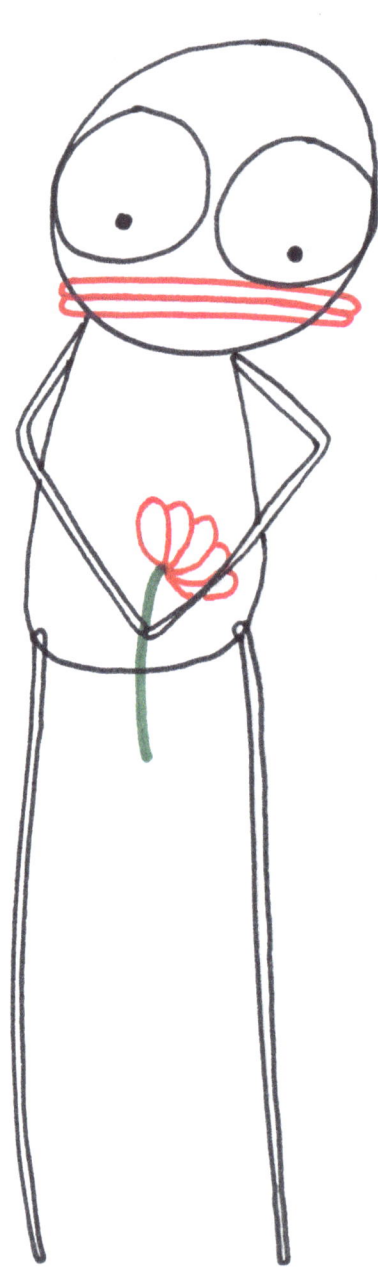

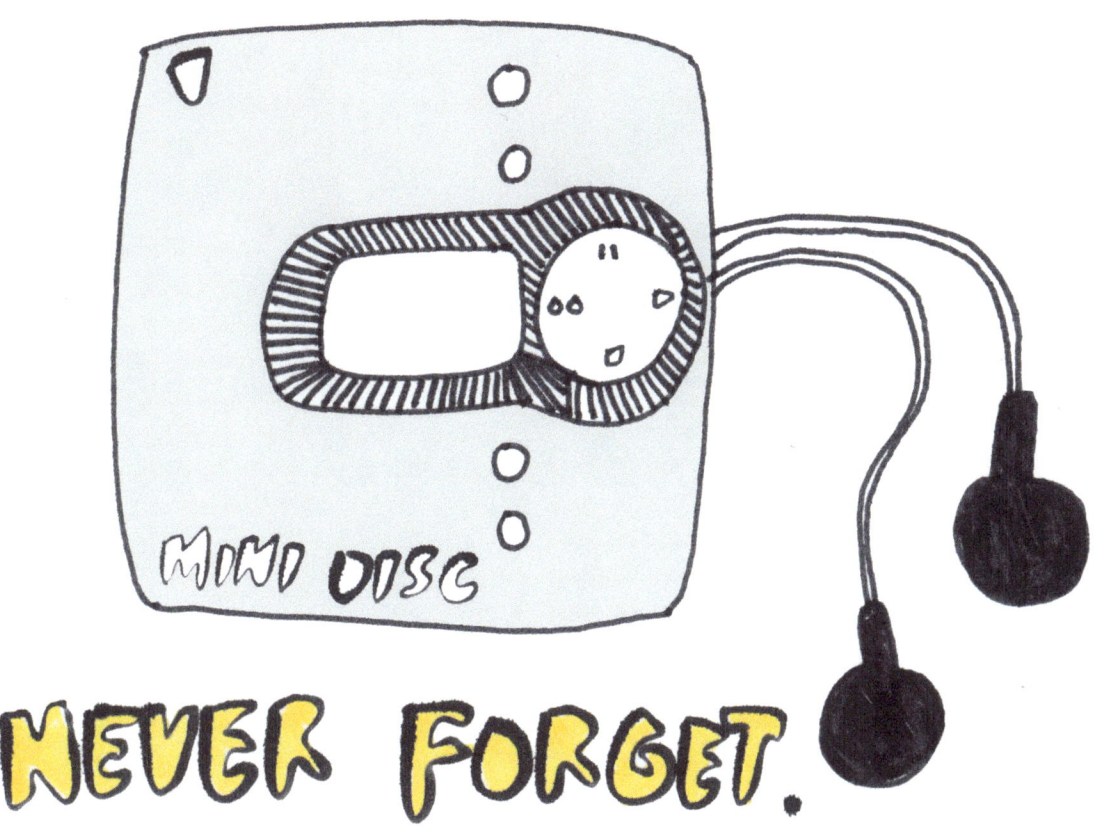

MINI DISC

NEVER FORGET.

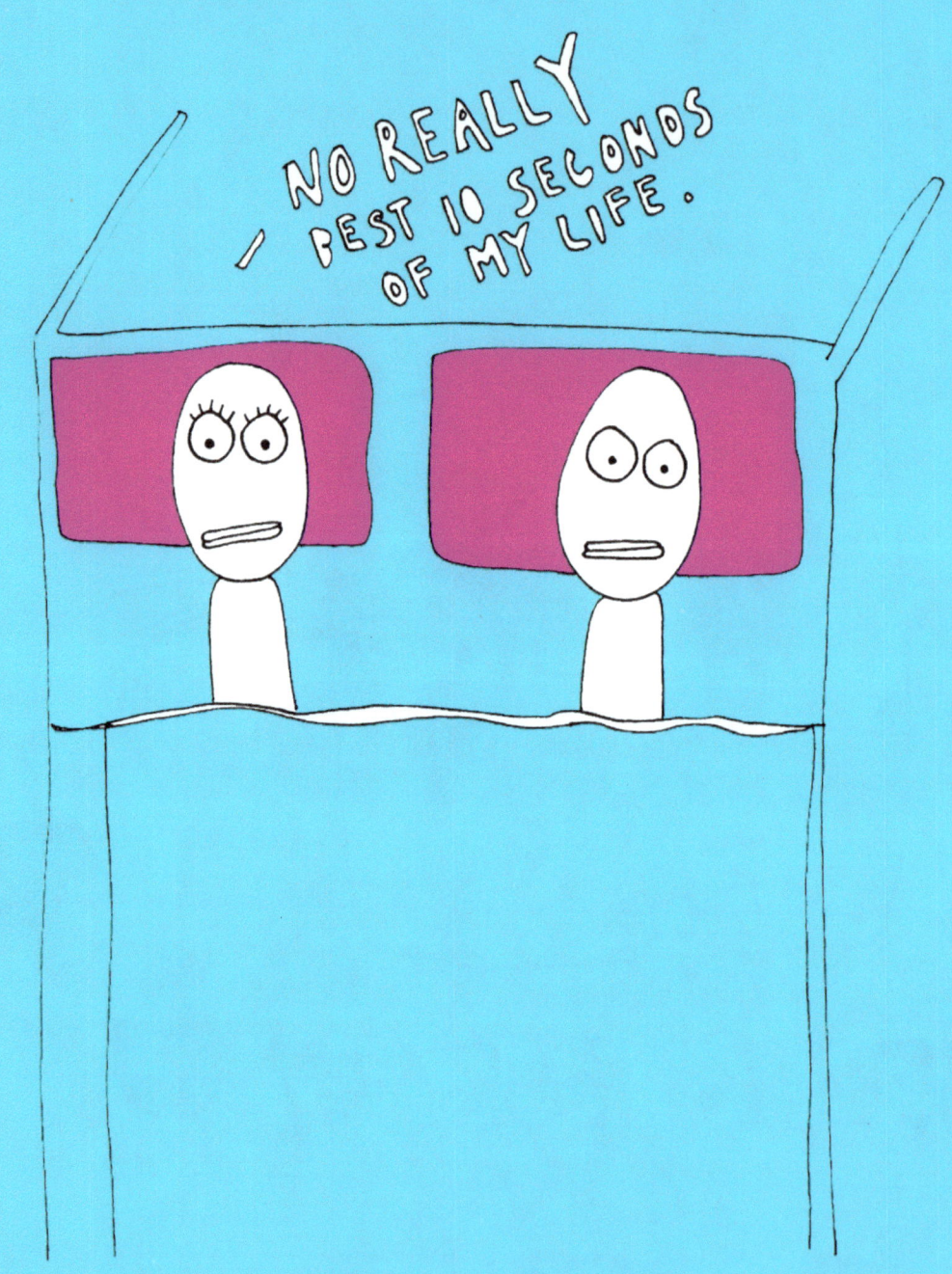

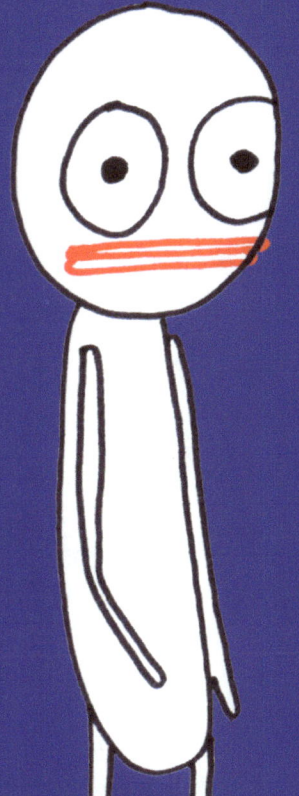

I FEEL CHEAP LAZY BROKE STARVED AND USED.

OCASIONALLY, WHEN LIFE REALLY SUCKED, SHE WOULD IMAGINE WHAT IT WAS LIKE TO BE DEAD.

SEEMED BORING.

PART 2
GET OVER
YOUR SELF.

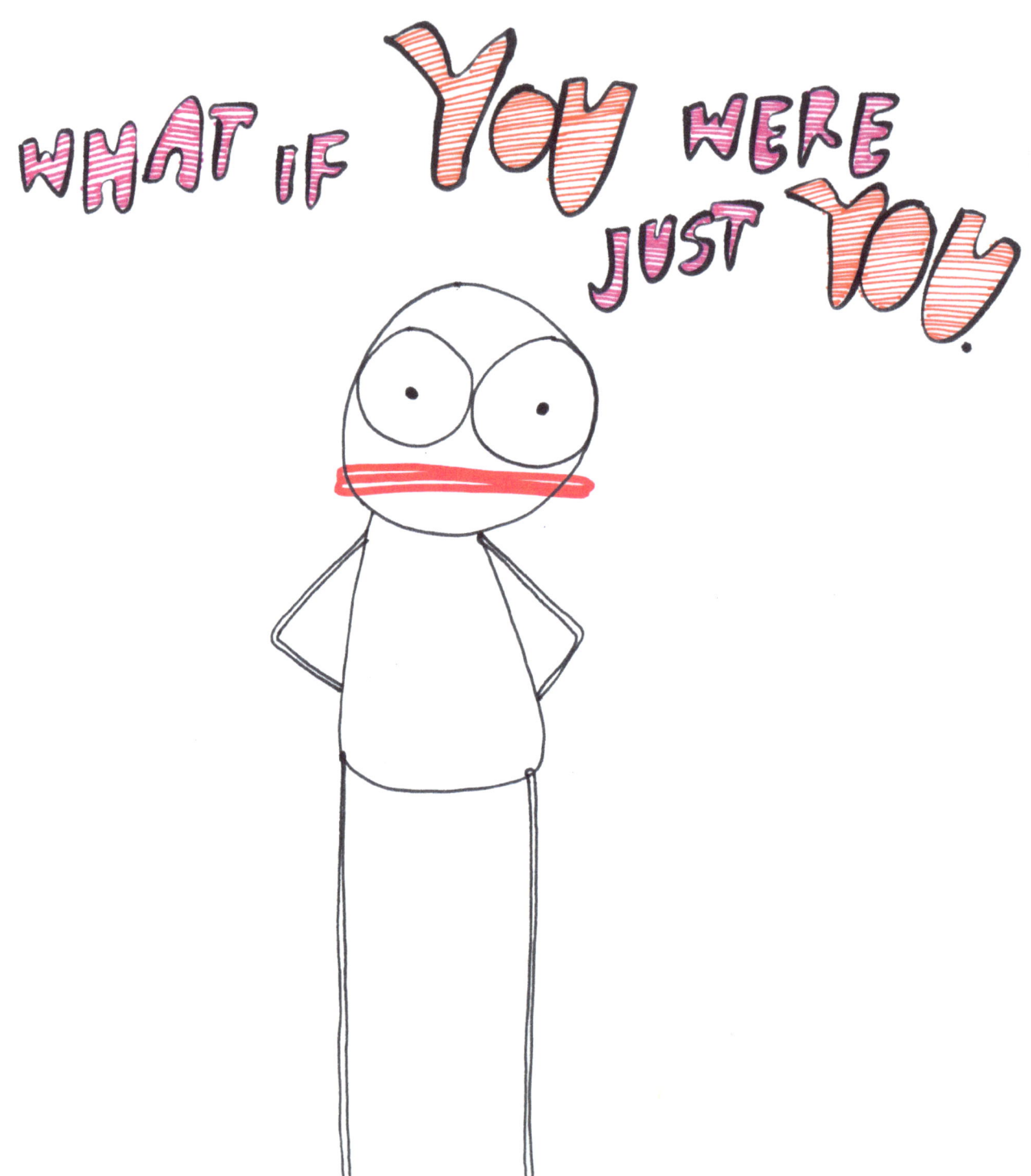

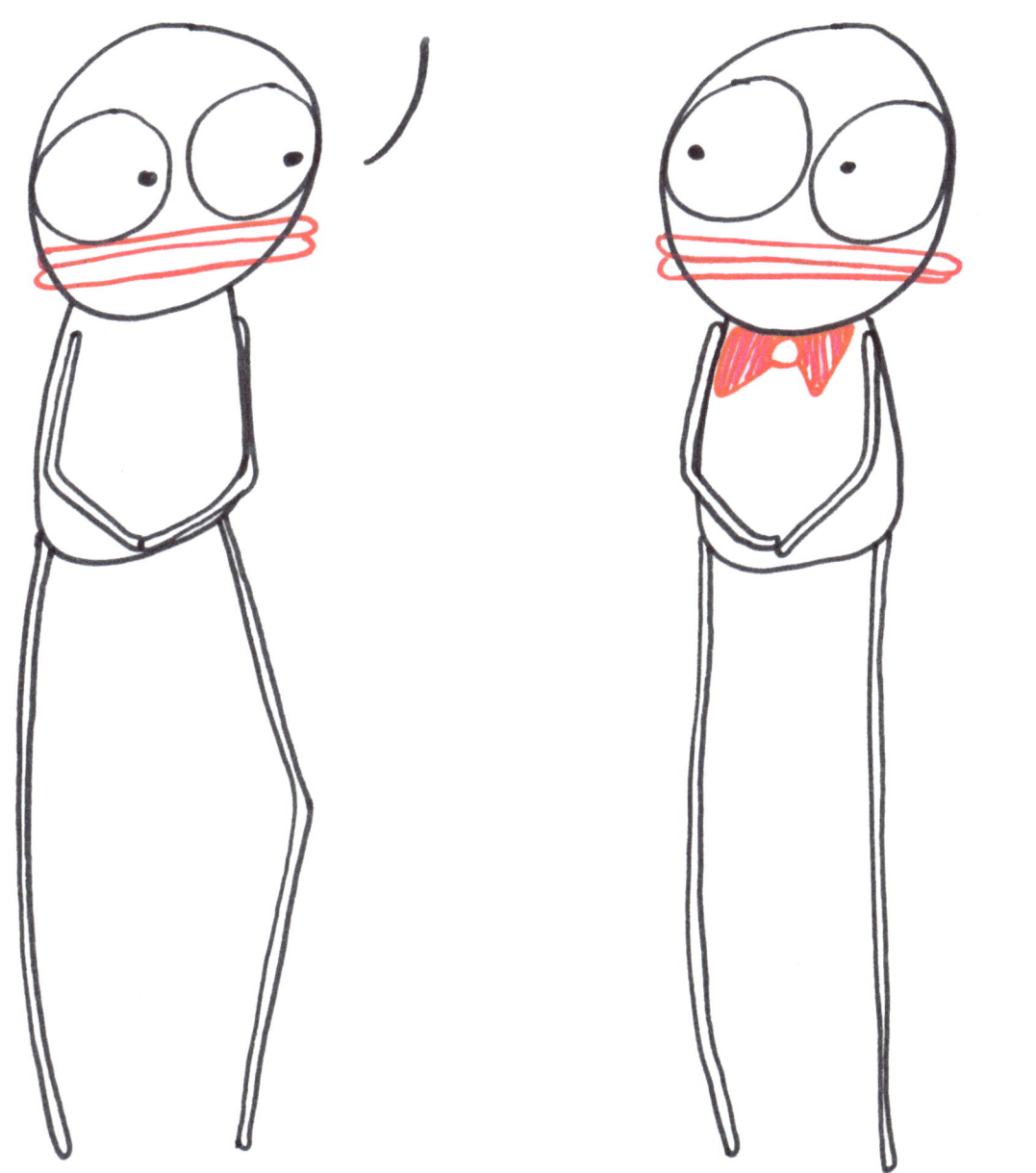

DONT GET MAD GET EVEN.

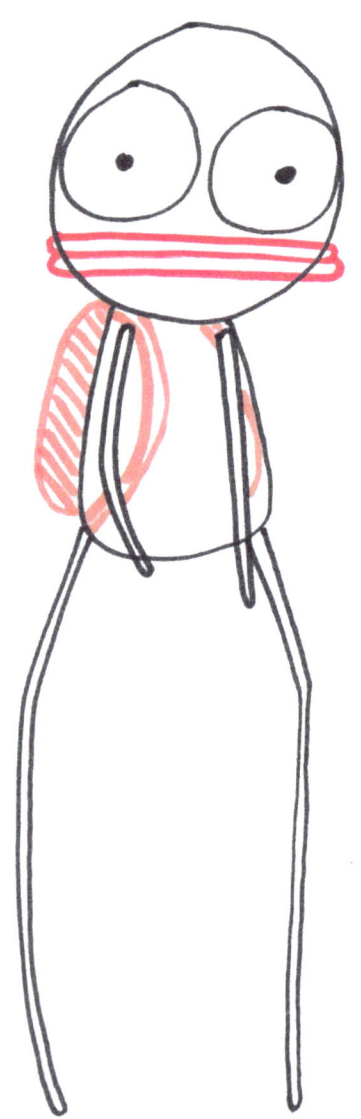

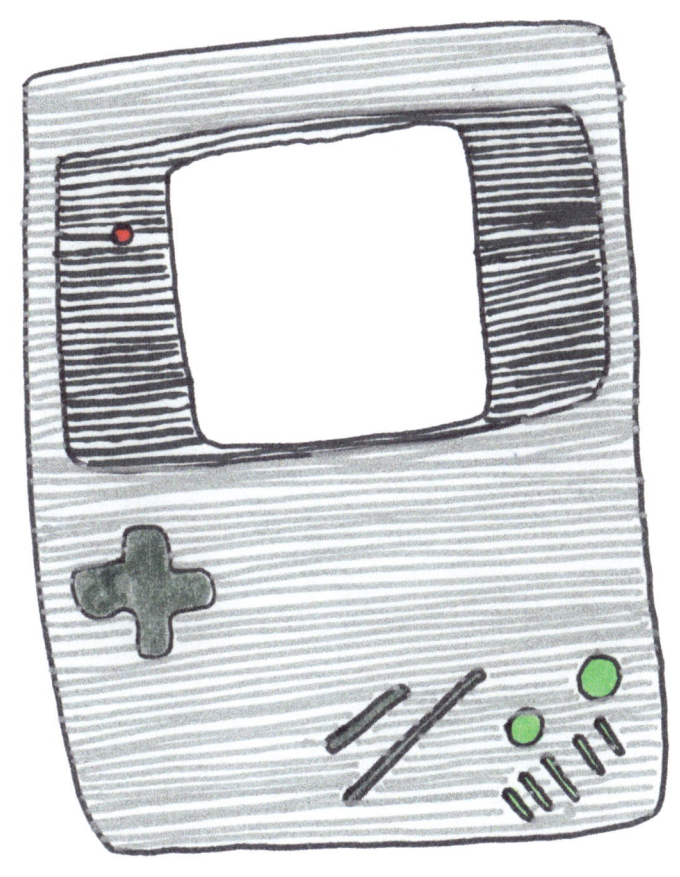

BRING GAMEBOY BACK.

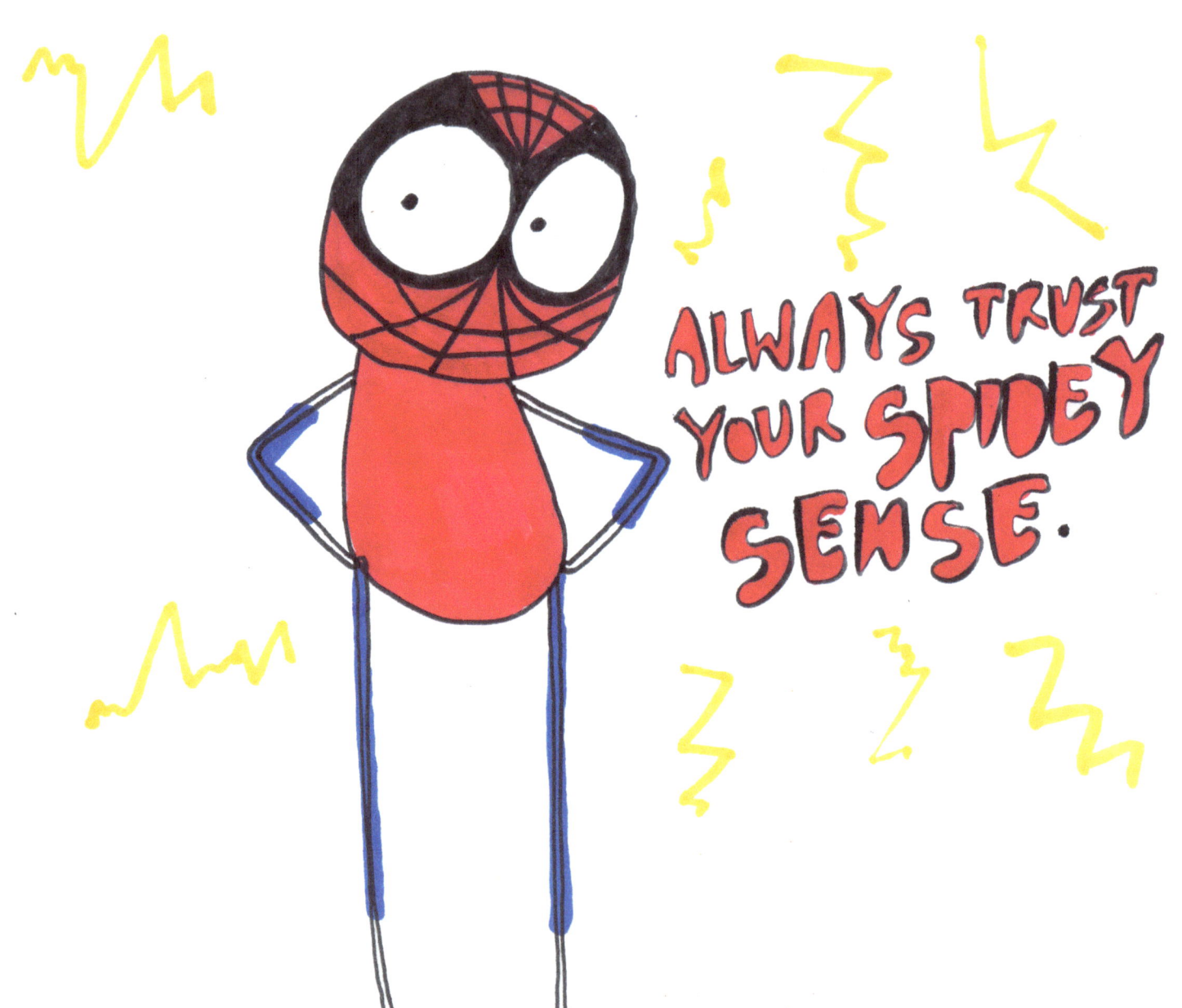

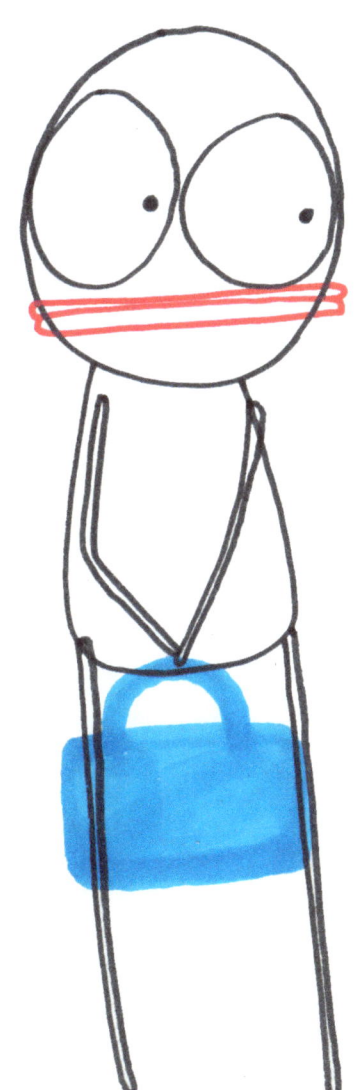
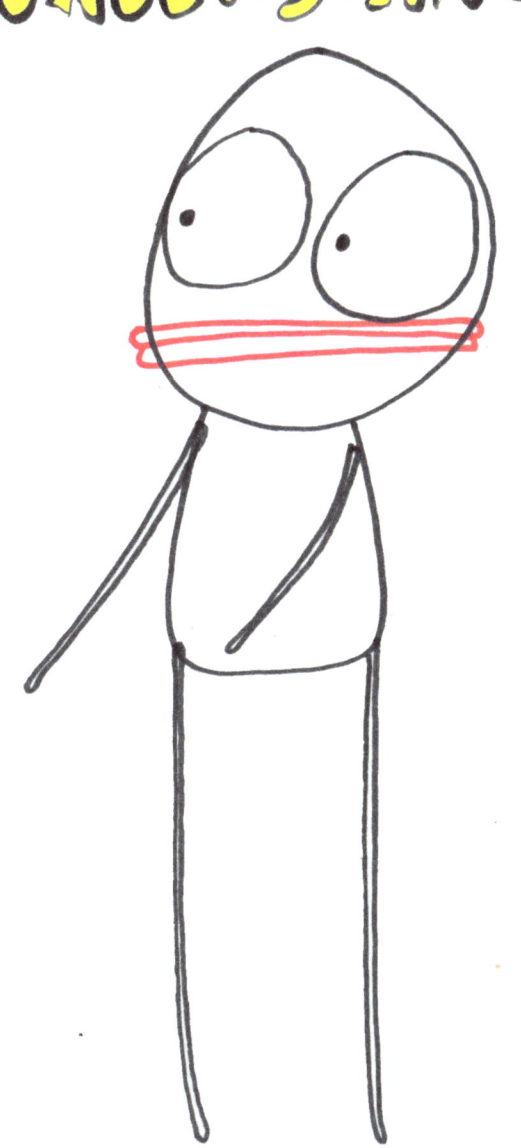

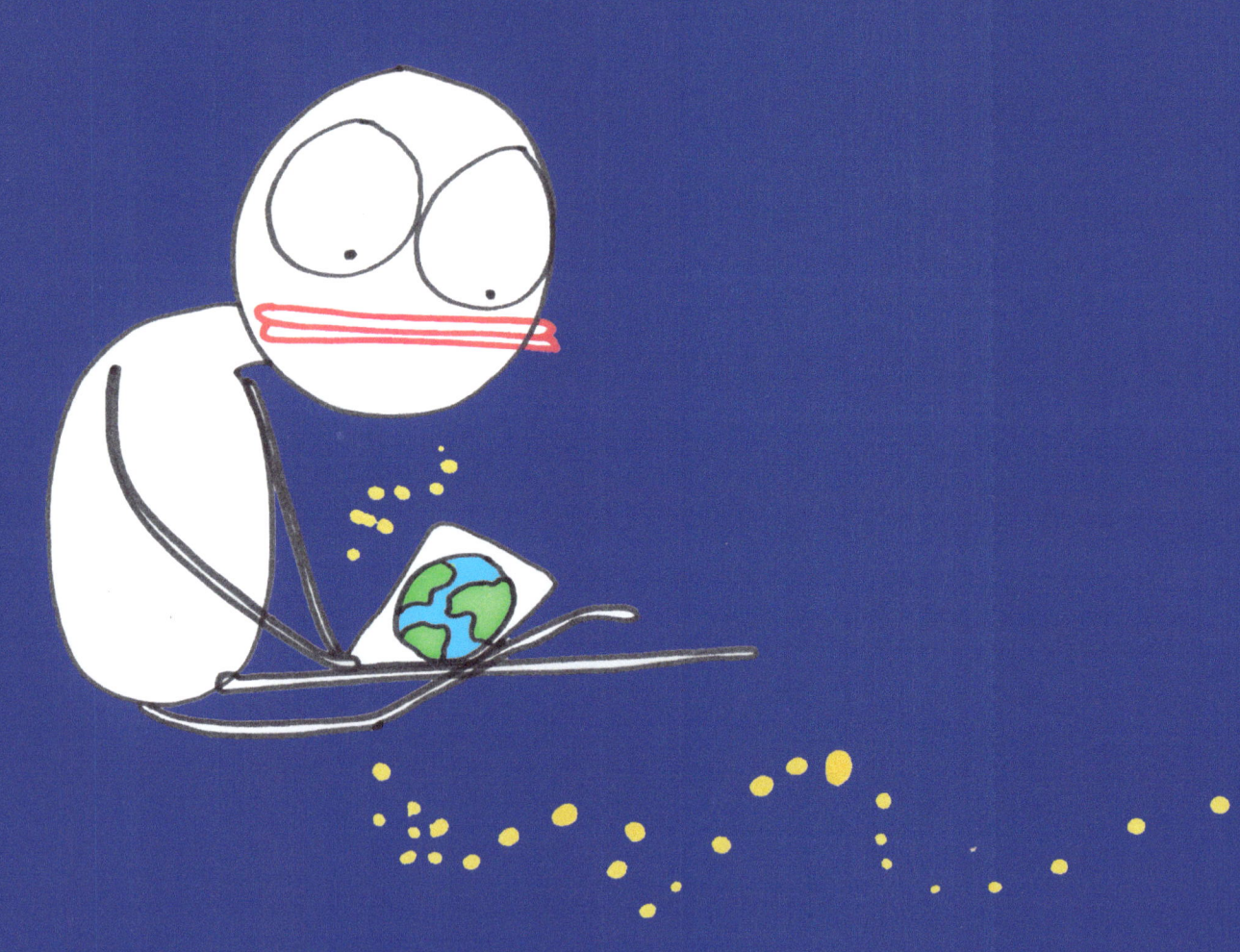

BRAINSTORMING PEACEFUL WAYS TO TAKE OVER THE WORLD.

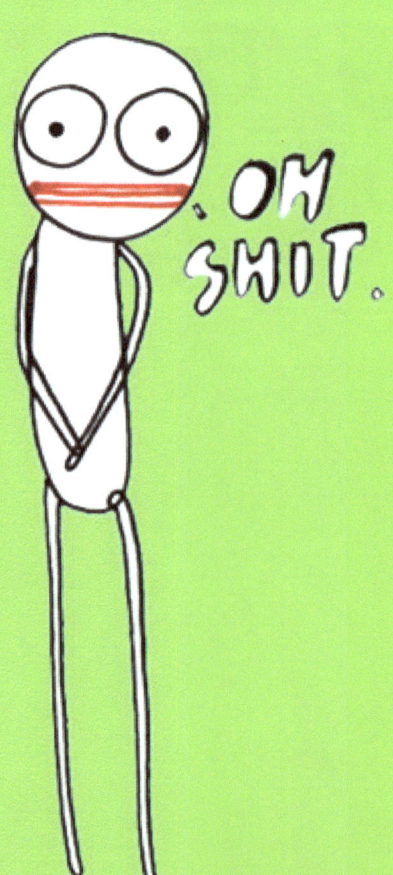

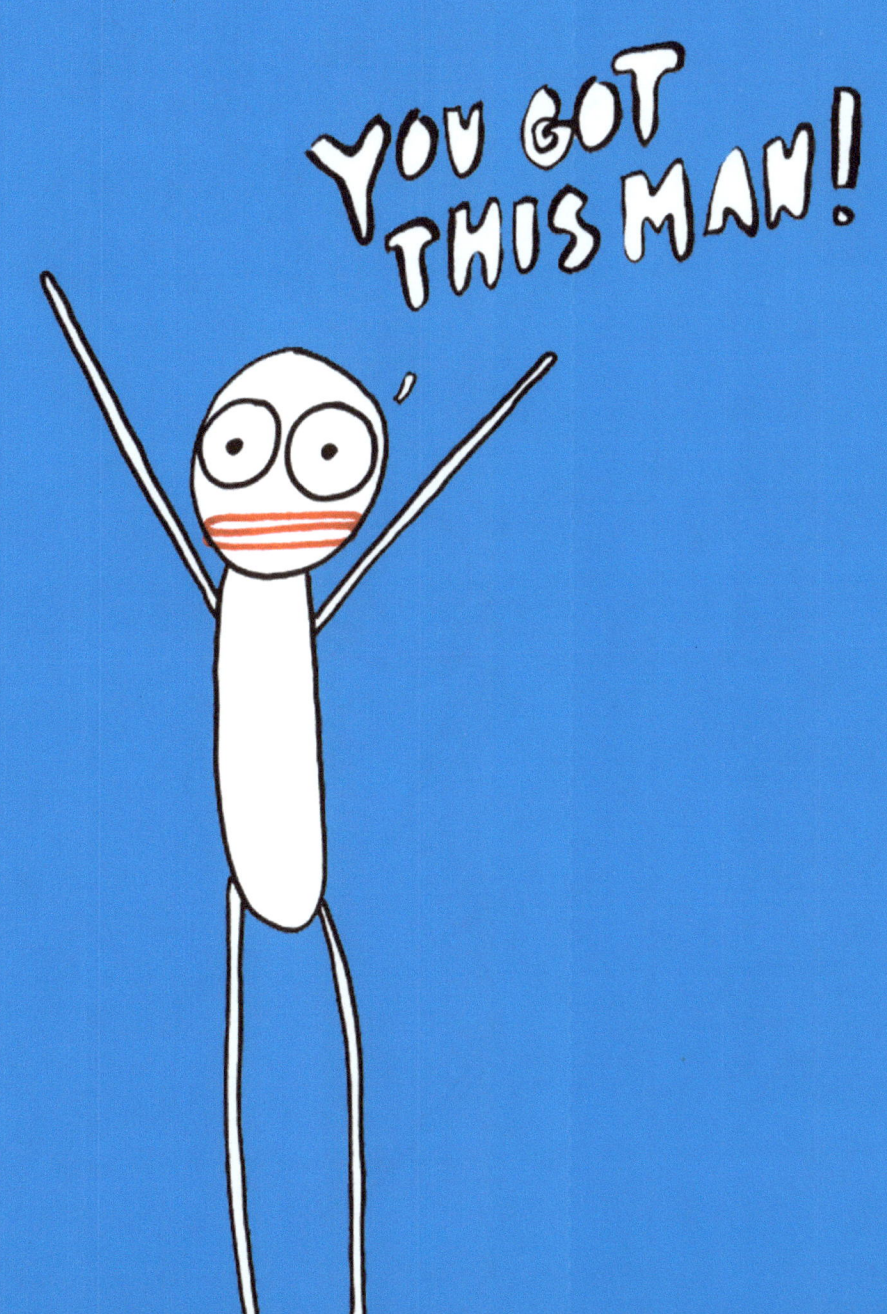

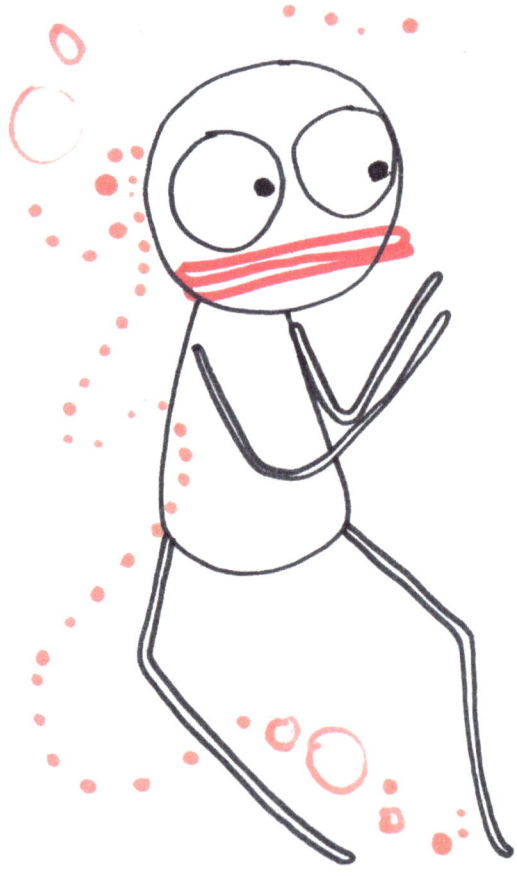

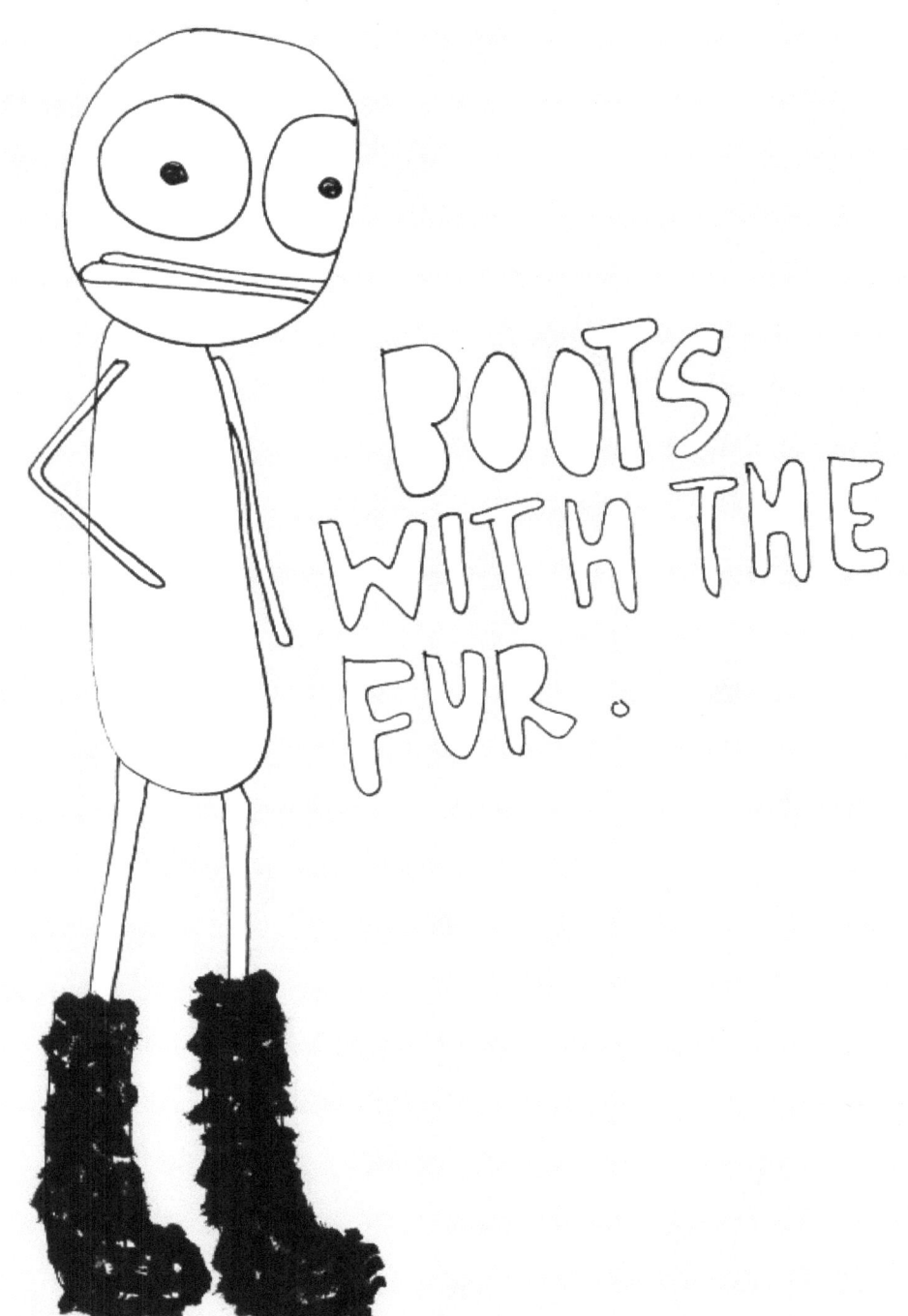

BOOTS WITH THE FUR.

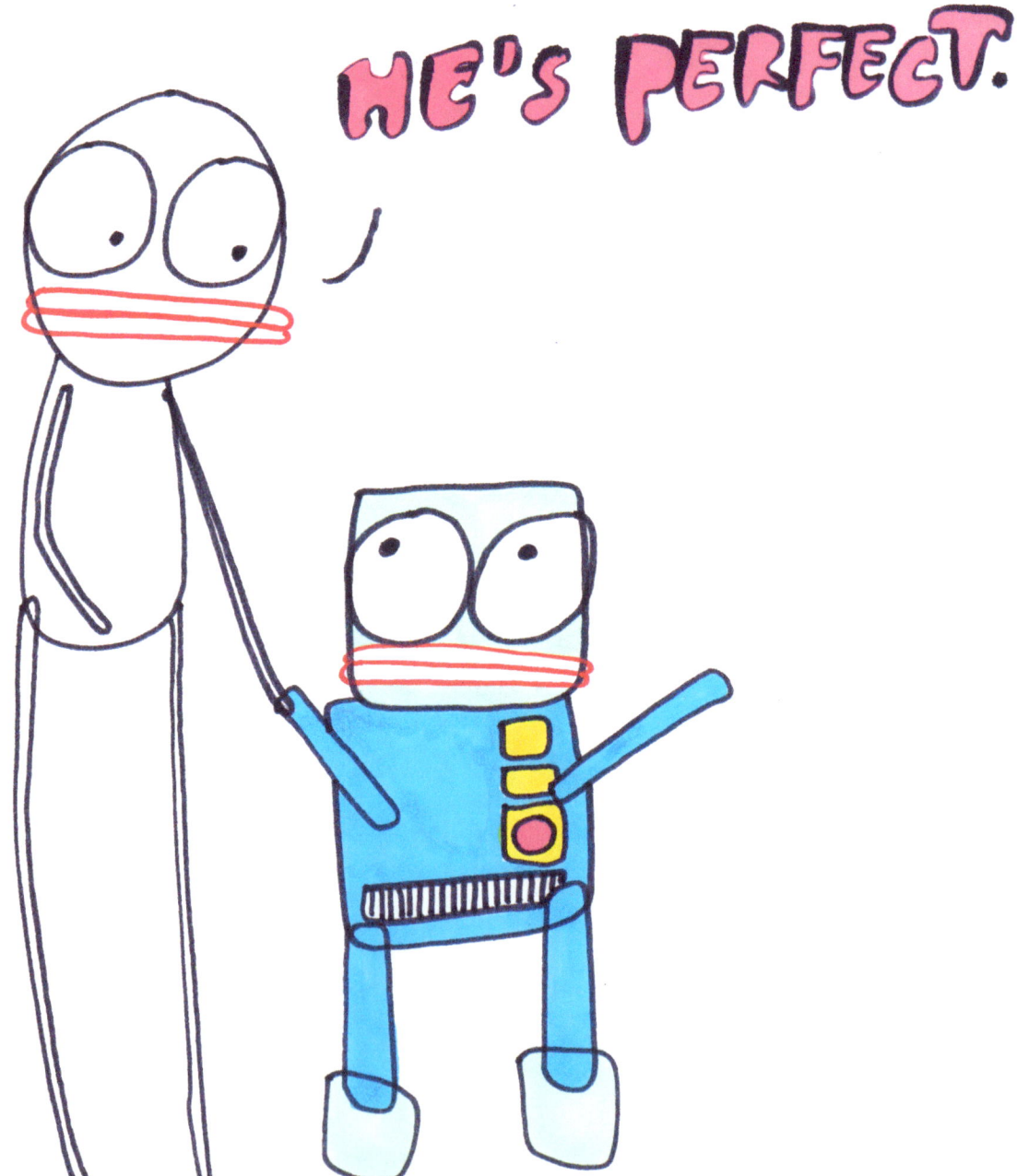

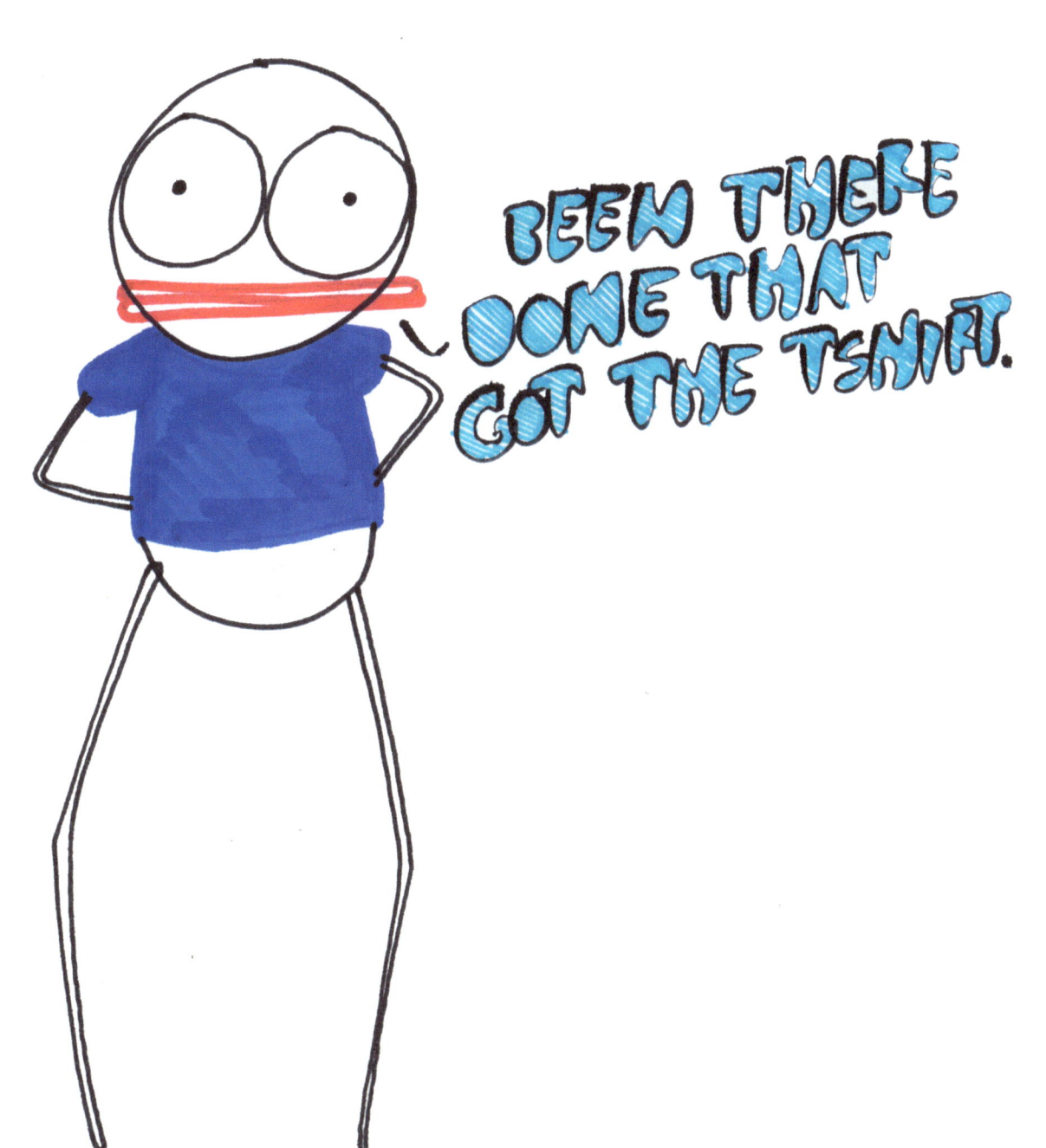

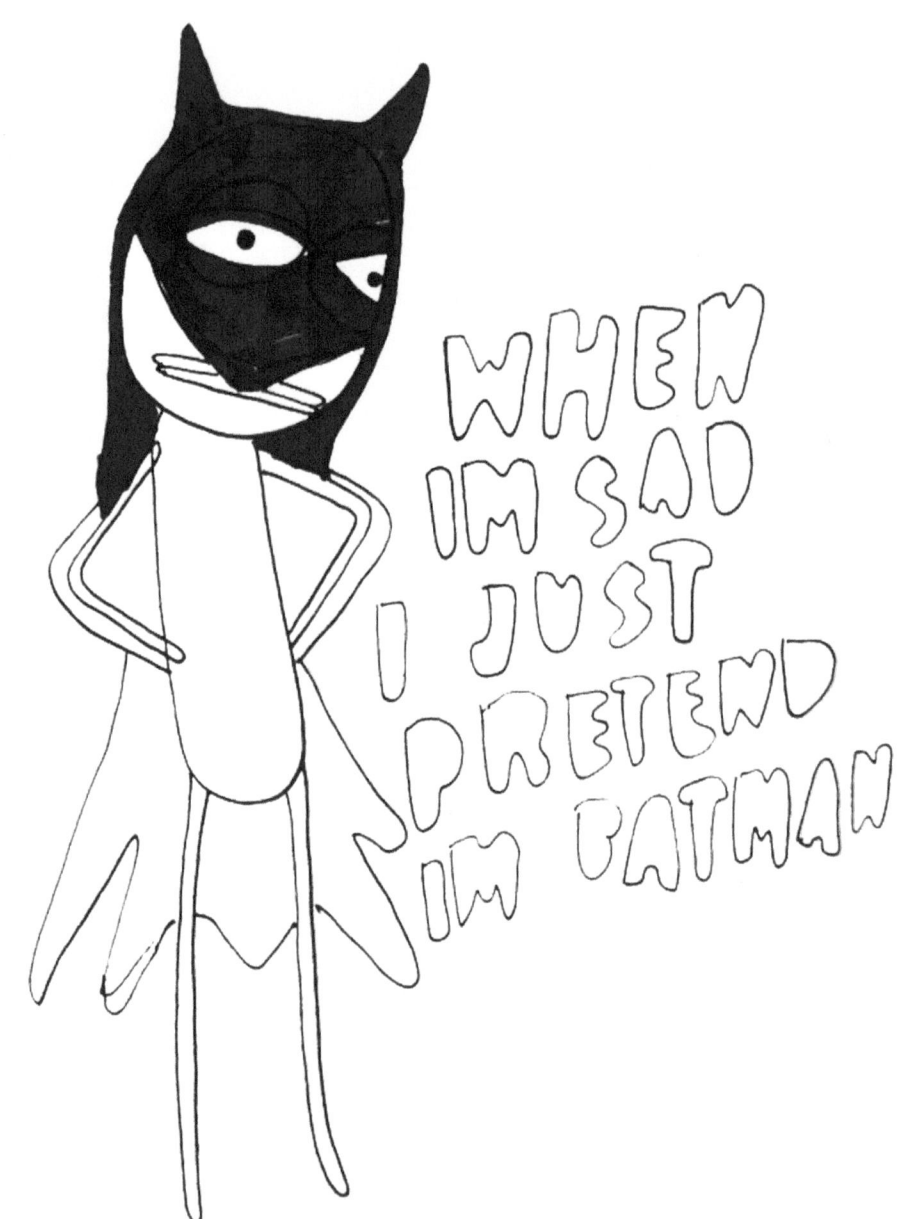

WHEN IM SAD I JUST PRETEND IM BATMAN

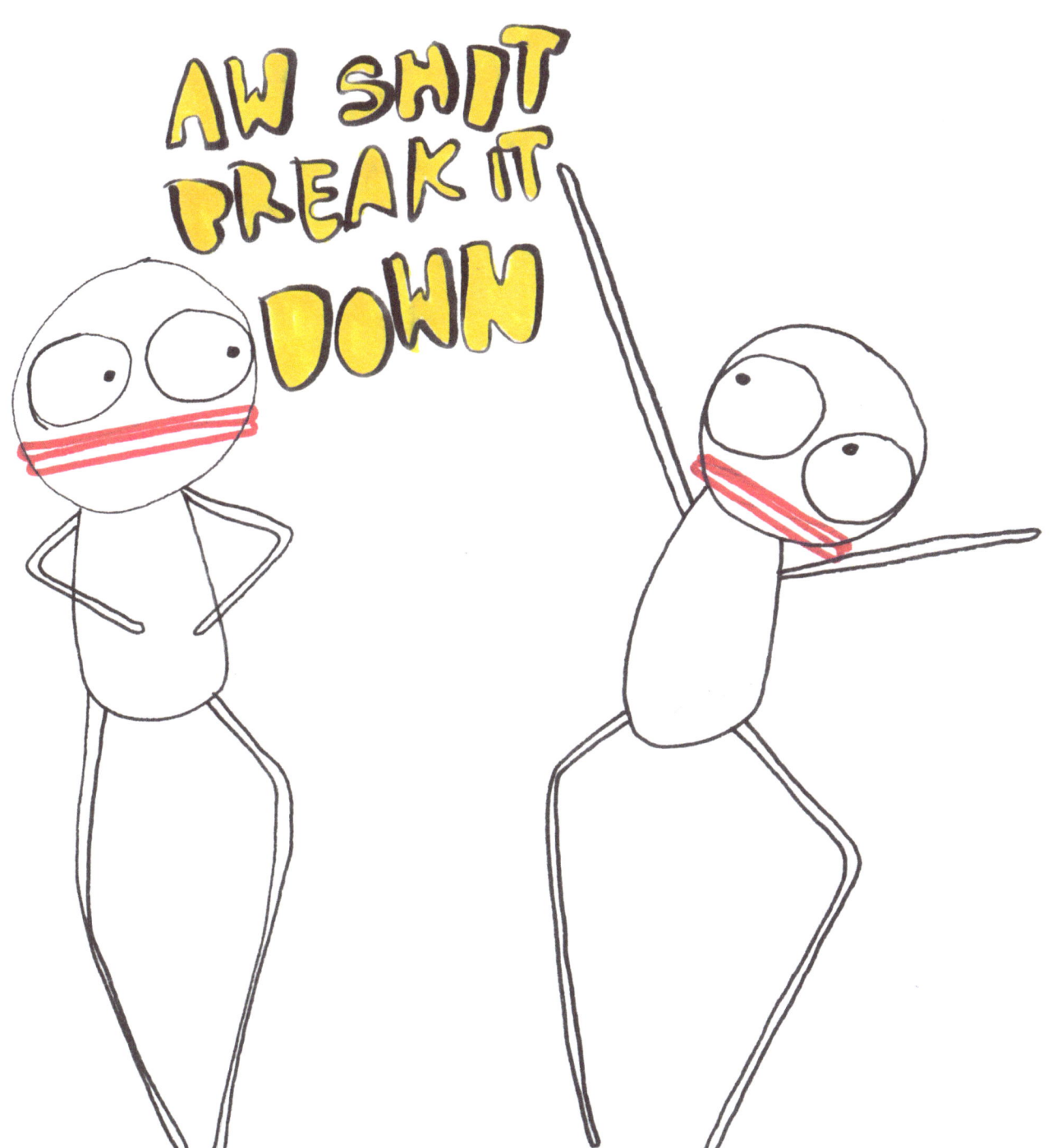

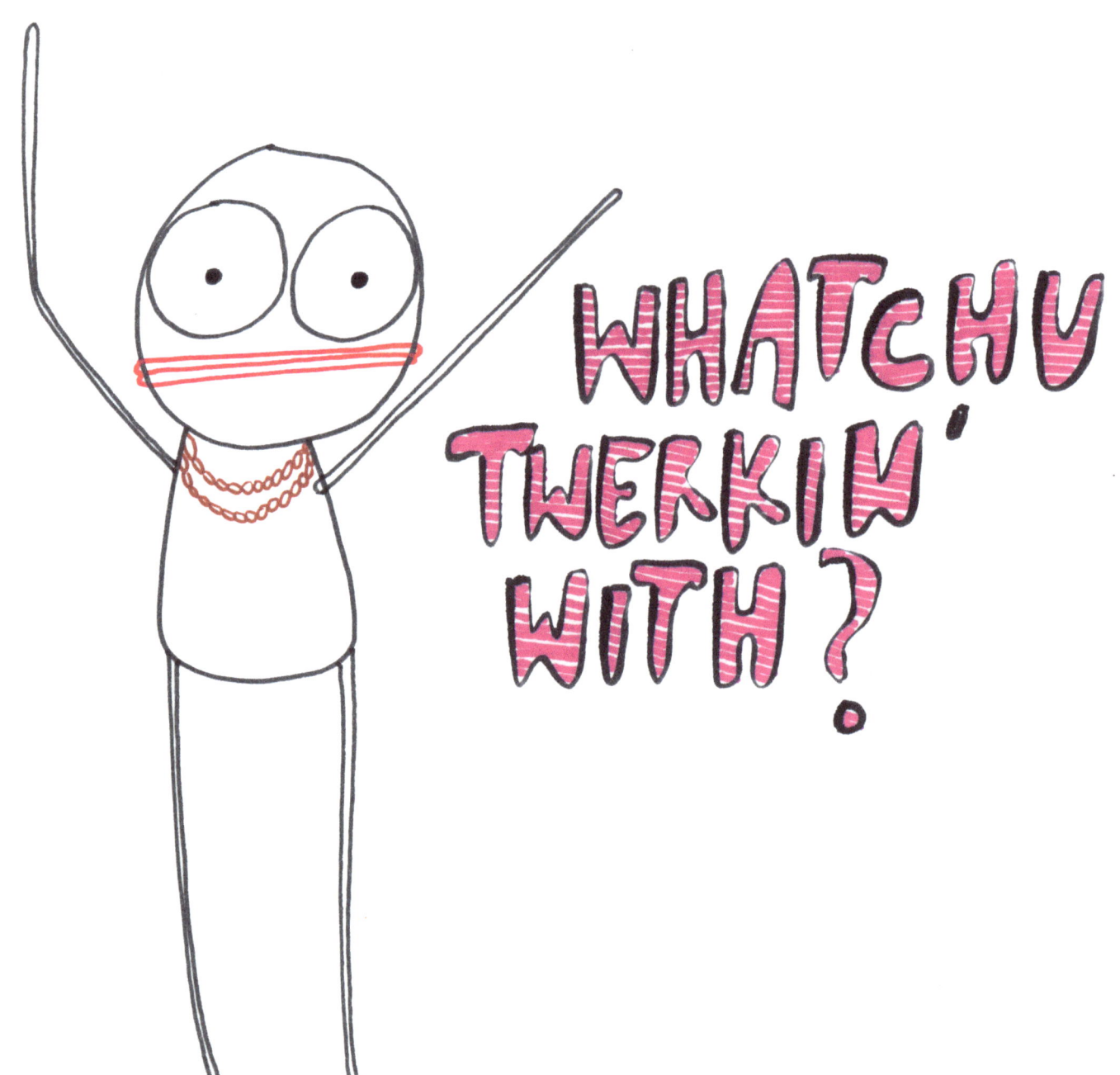

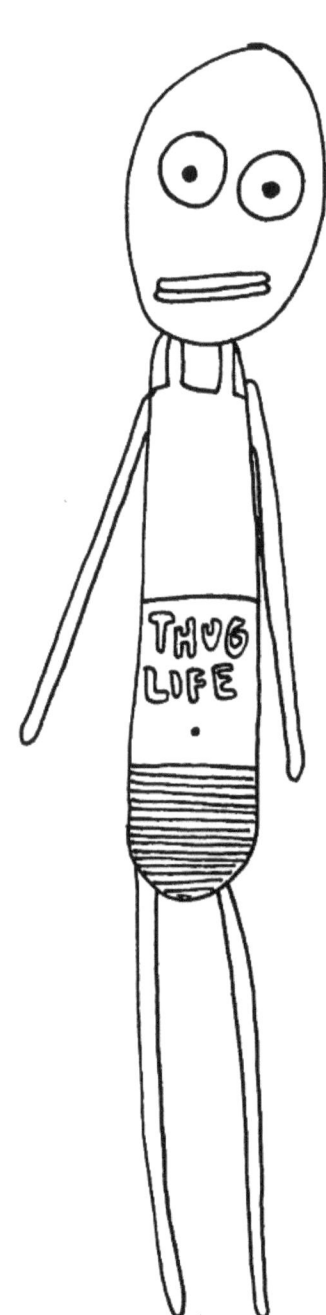

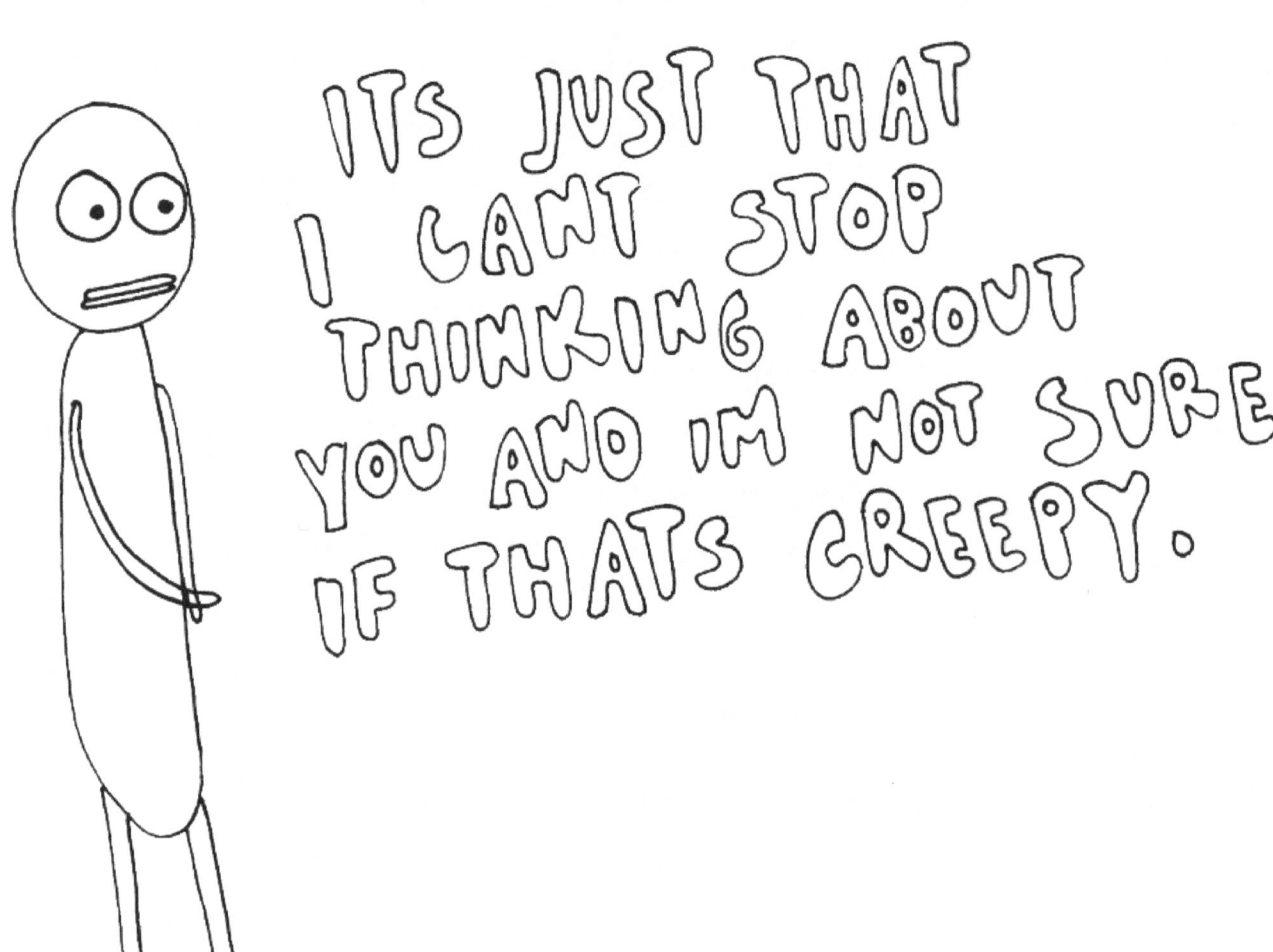

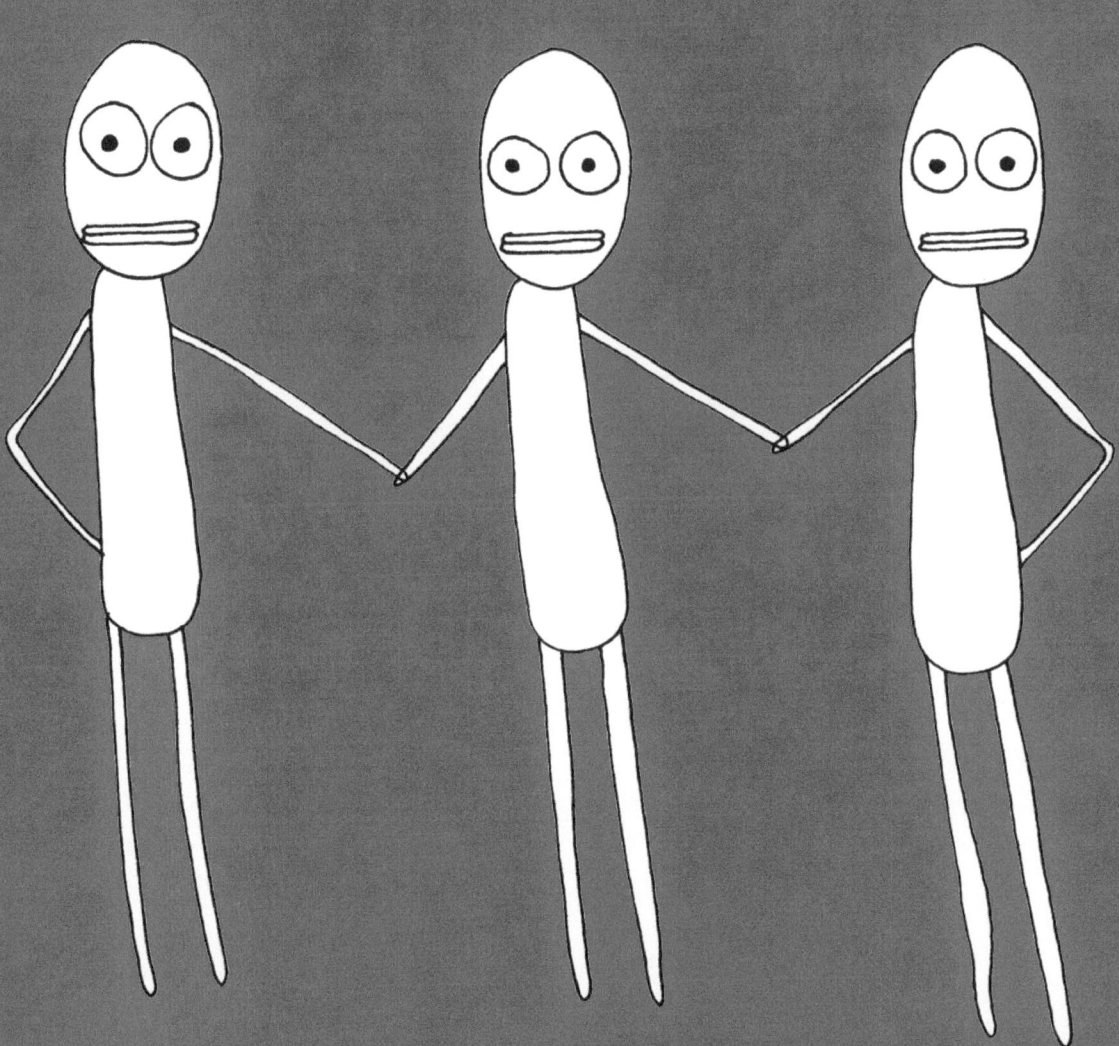

THINGS WOULD NEVER BE PERFECT, BUT HE WAS AND ALWAYS WOULD BE THE MOST BEAUTIFUL THING SHE HAD EVER SEEN.

PART 3
THIS MEANS
I LOVE YOU.

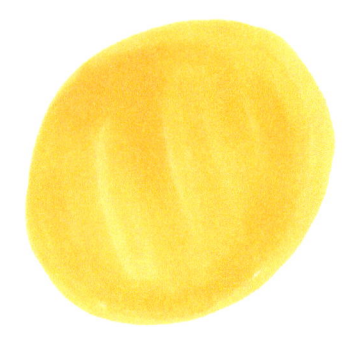
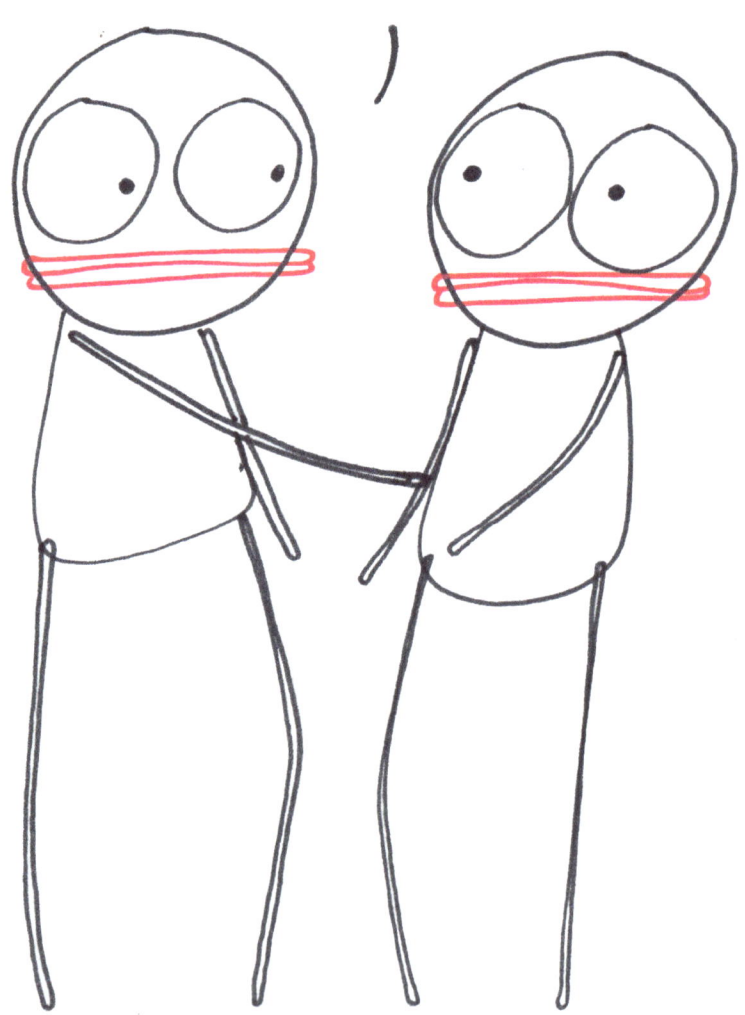

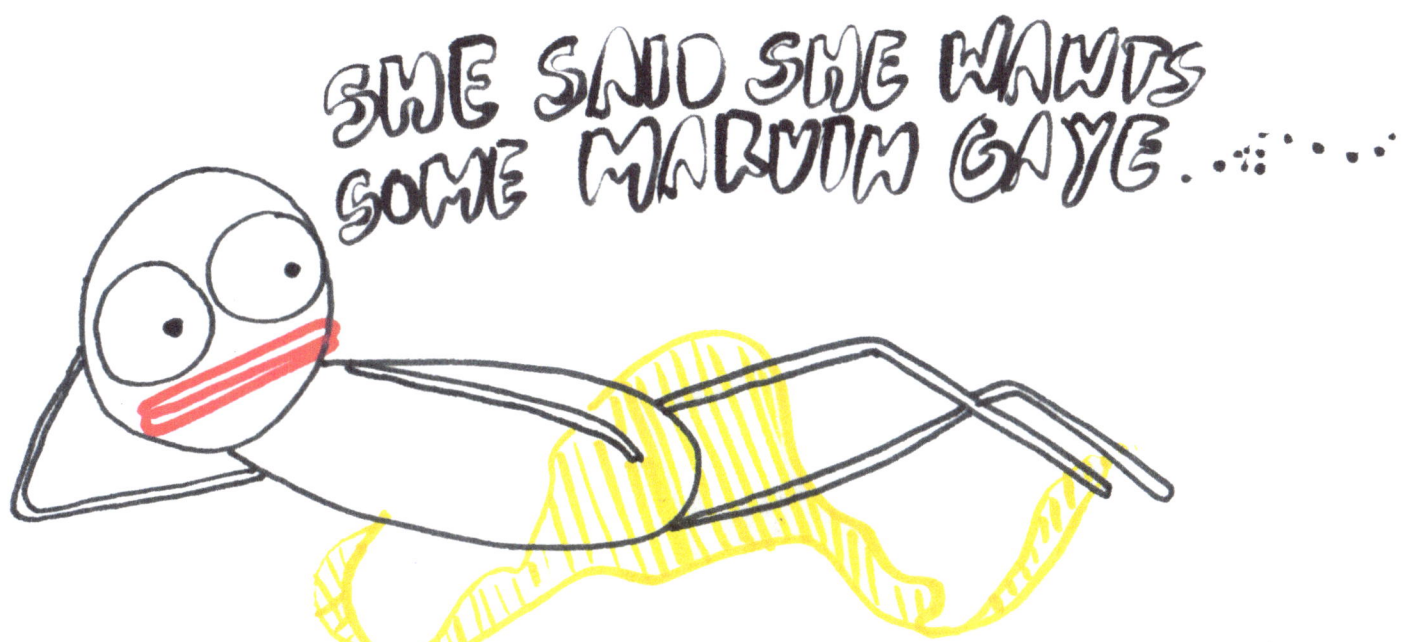

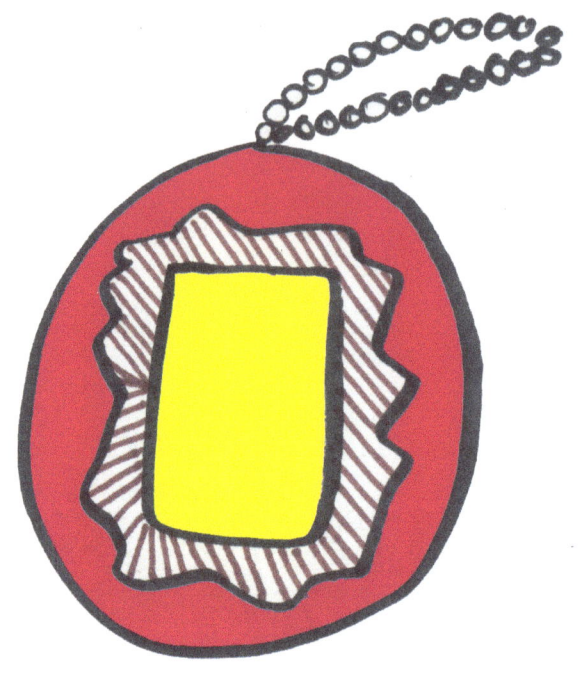

ILL NEVER LOVE
ANYONE LIKE
I DID MY
TAMOGATCHI.

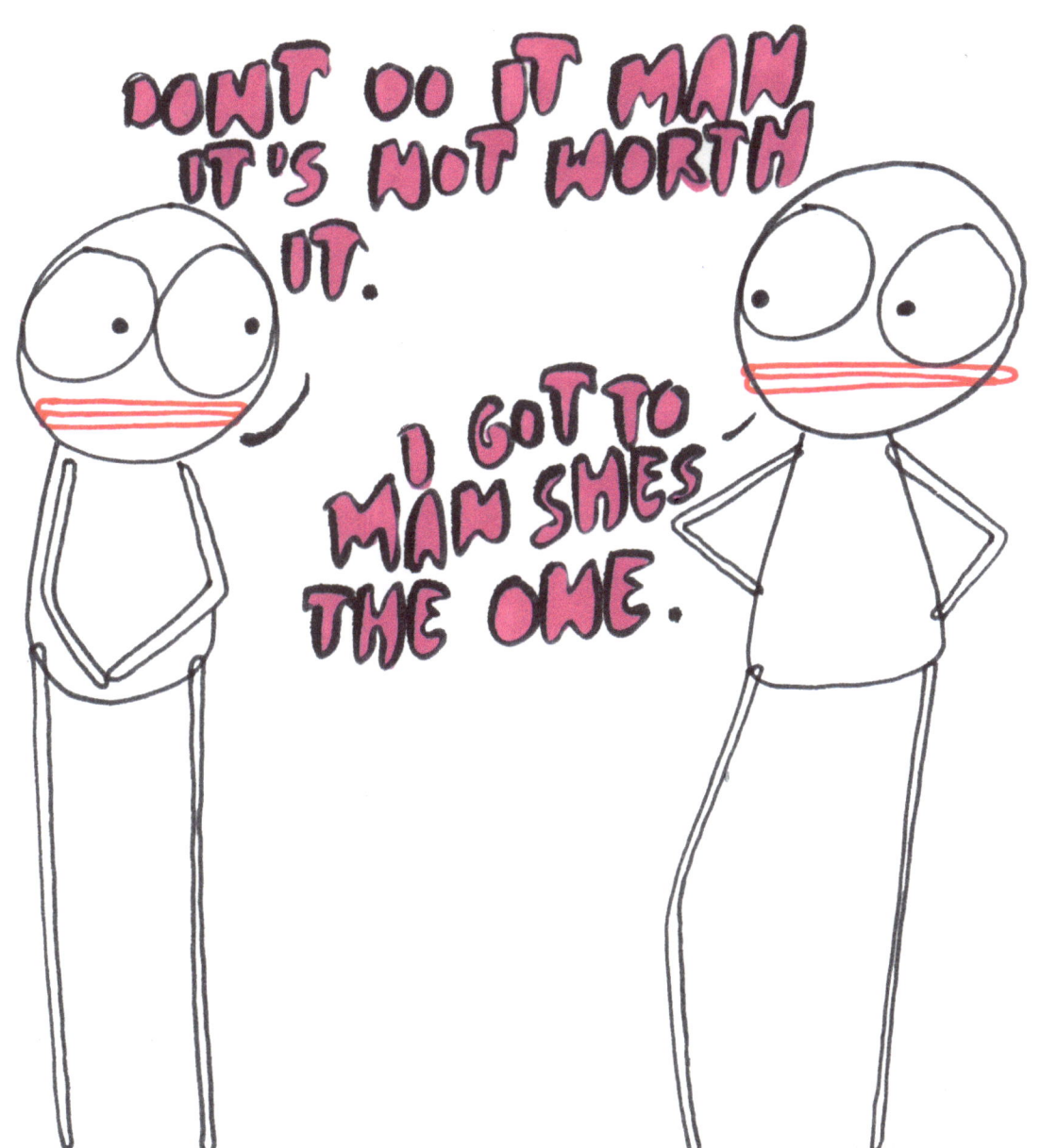

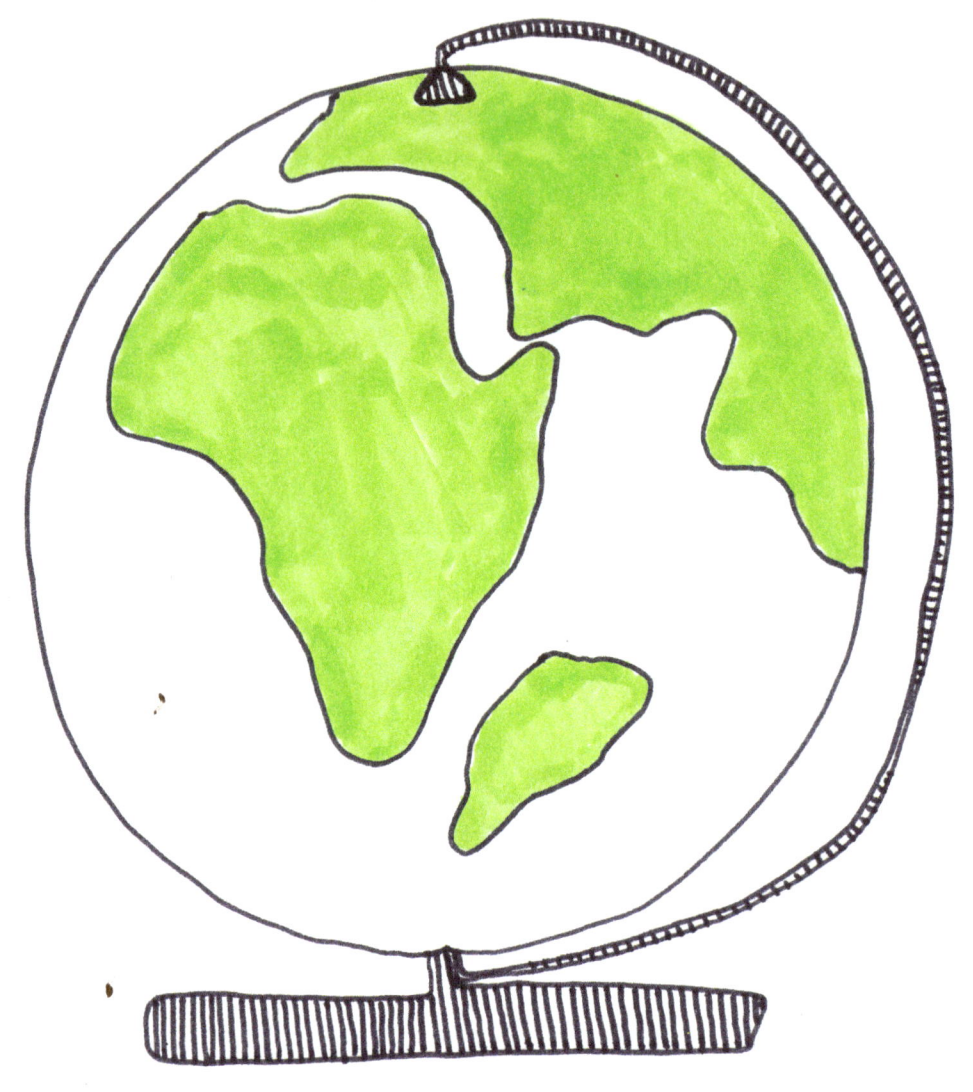

I LOVE HIM BECAUSE OF ALL OF THESE
LITTLE THINGS WHICH ENDS UP BEING
THE BIGGEST THING IN THE ENTIRE WORLD.

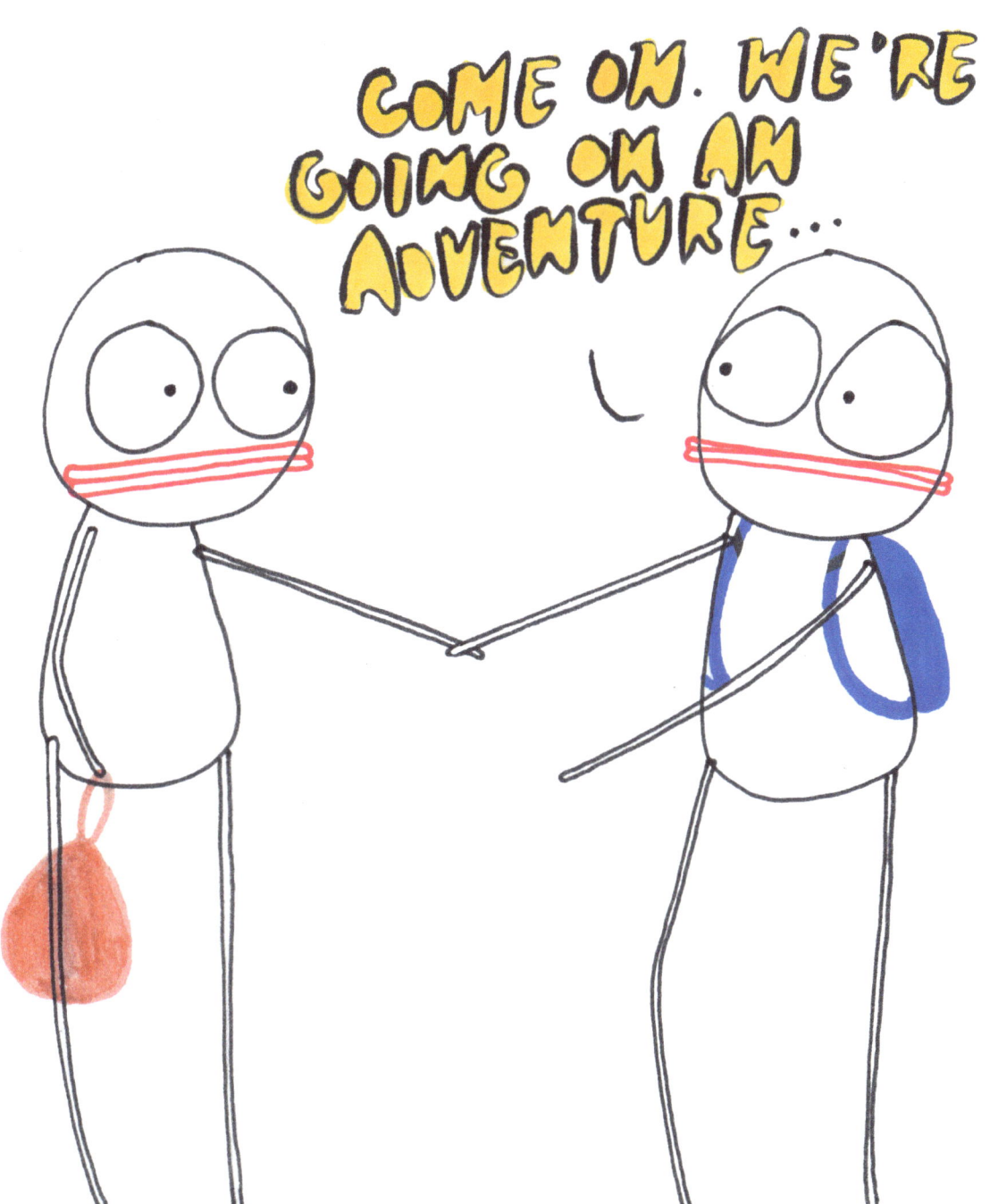

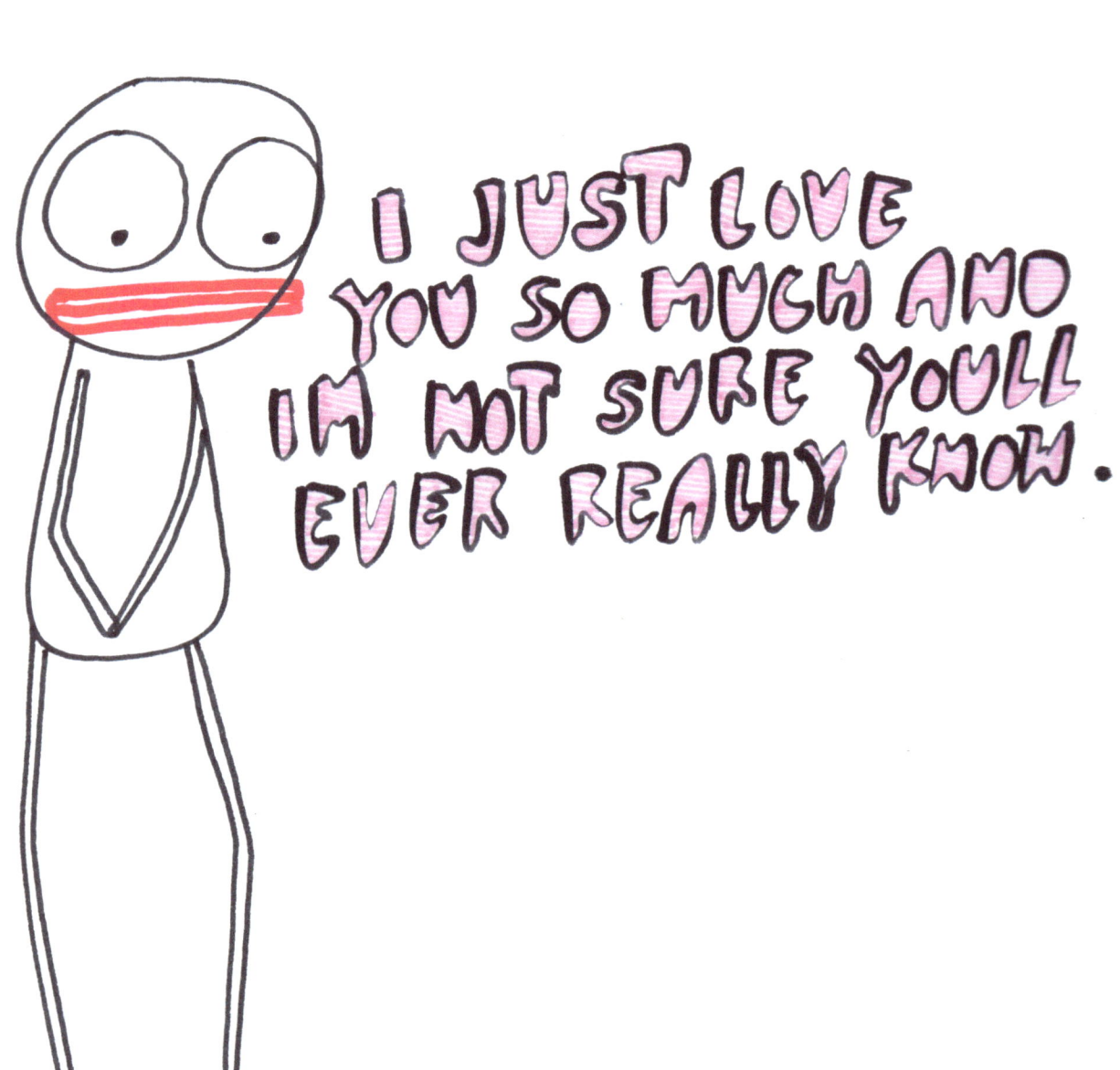

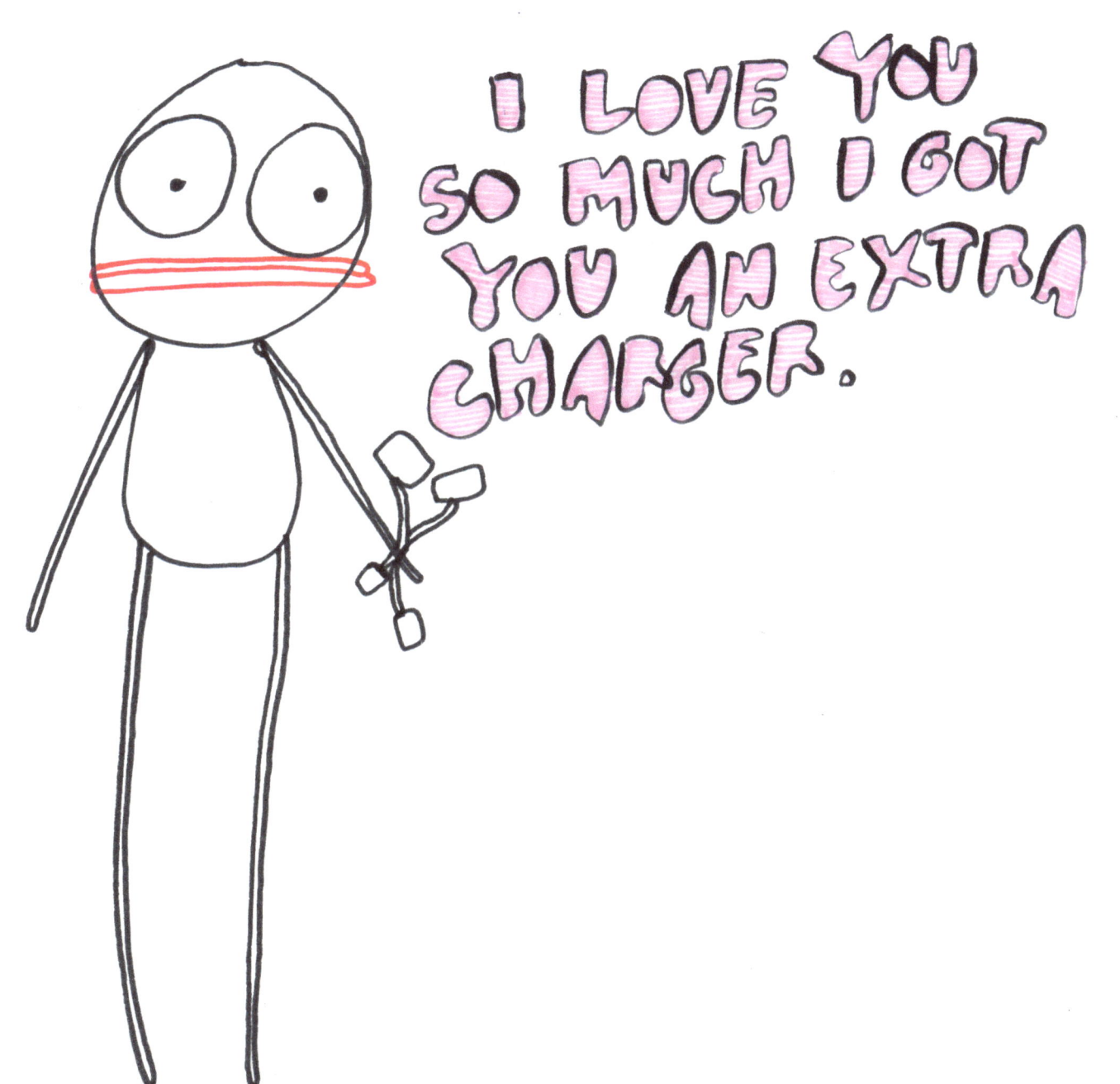

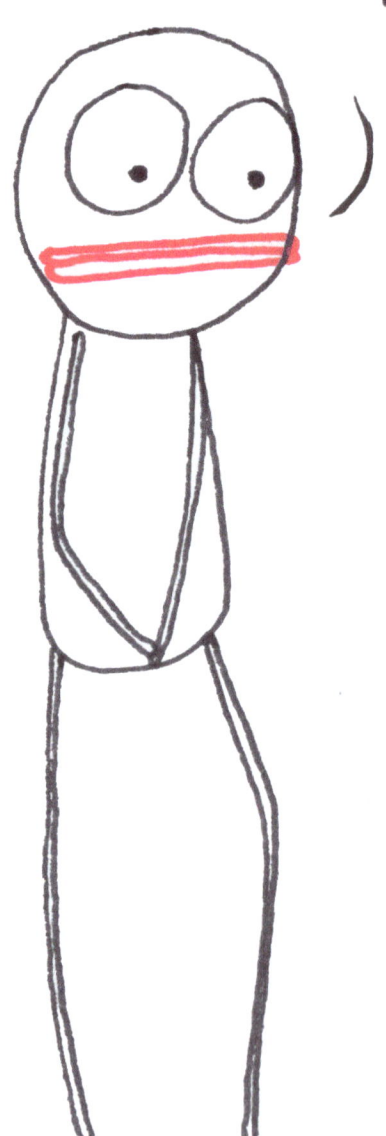

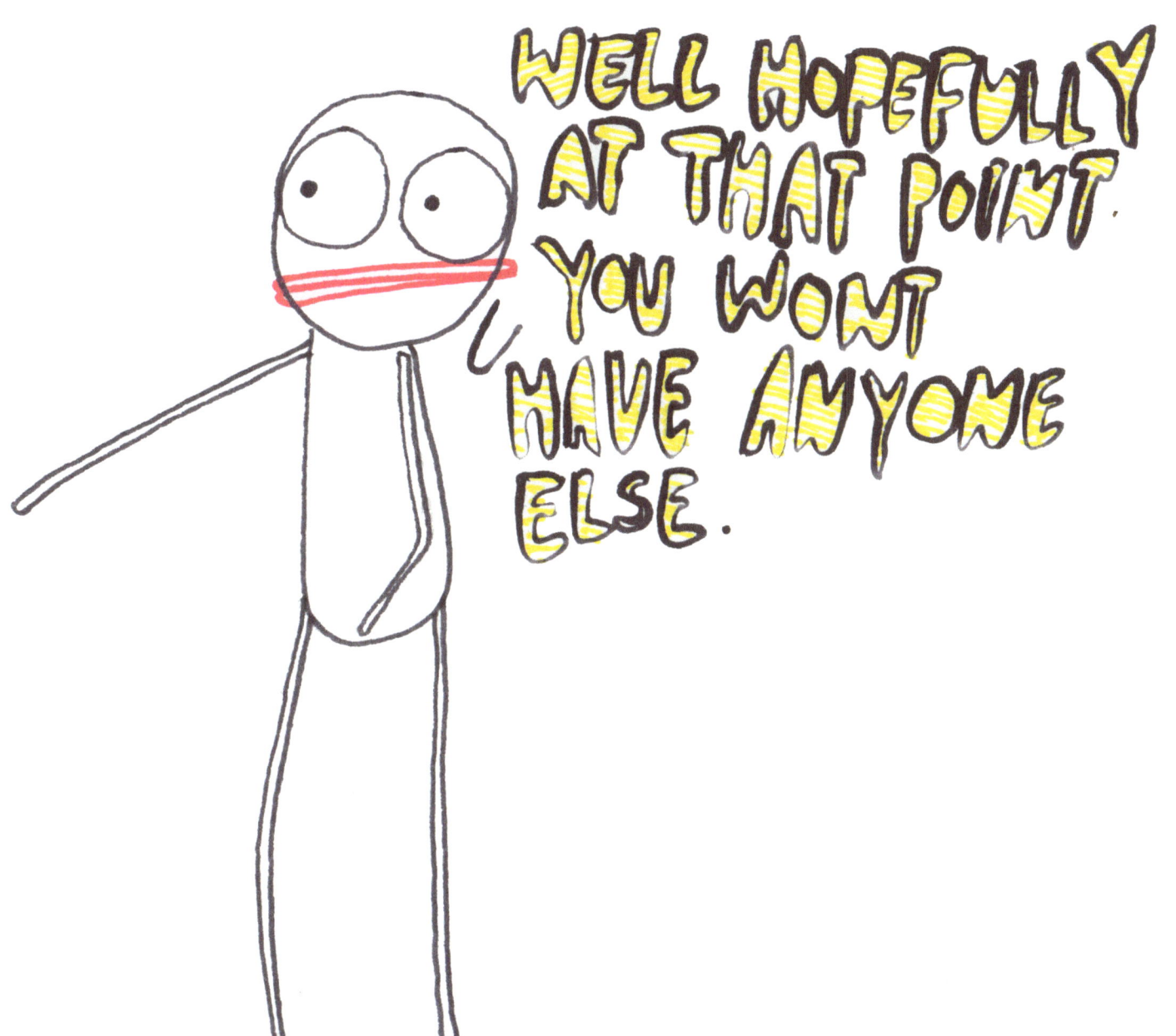

MAGIC EXISTS ONLY WHEN YOU BELIEVE IN IT.

SOMETHING ABOUT HIM WAS ALWAYS SO MAGICAL.

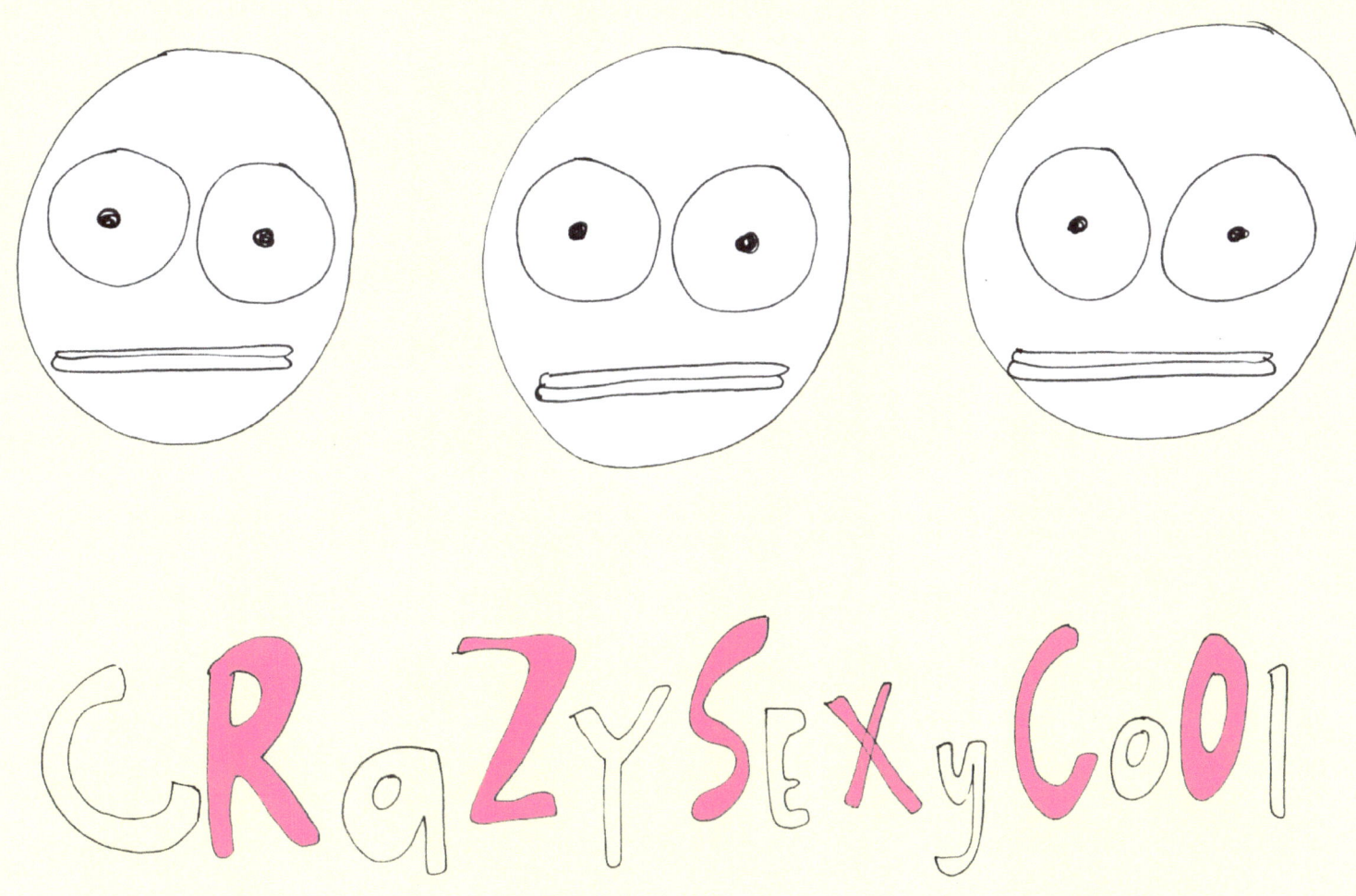

IM NOT SURE WHAT I INVISIONED, PUT DEFINITELY DIFFERENT THAN WHAT IT IS. EITHER WAY WHAT WILL BE WILL ALWAYS BE AND THE REST WILL PE HISTORY.

PART 4
THE MEANING
OF LIFE.

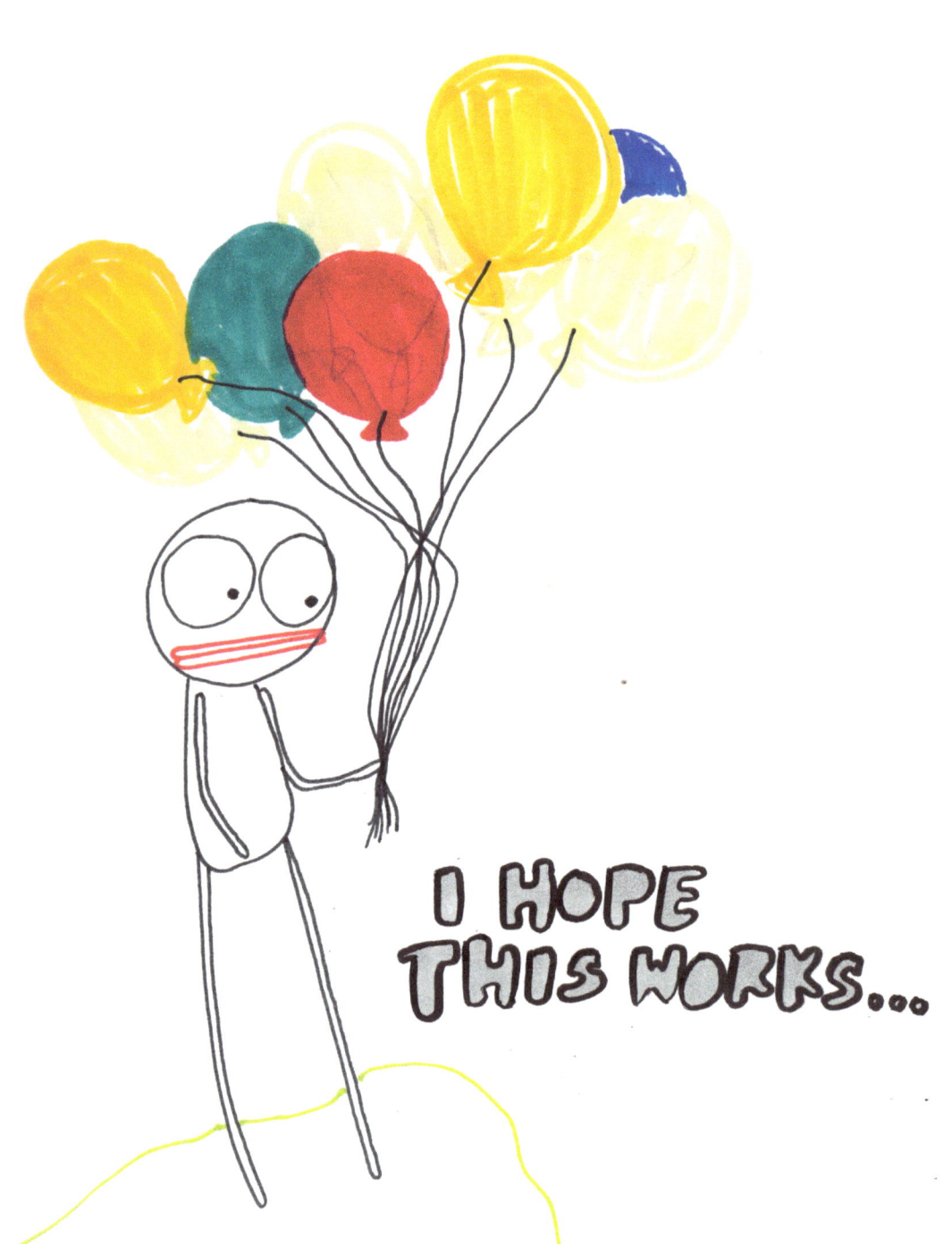

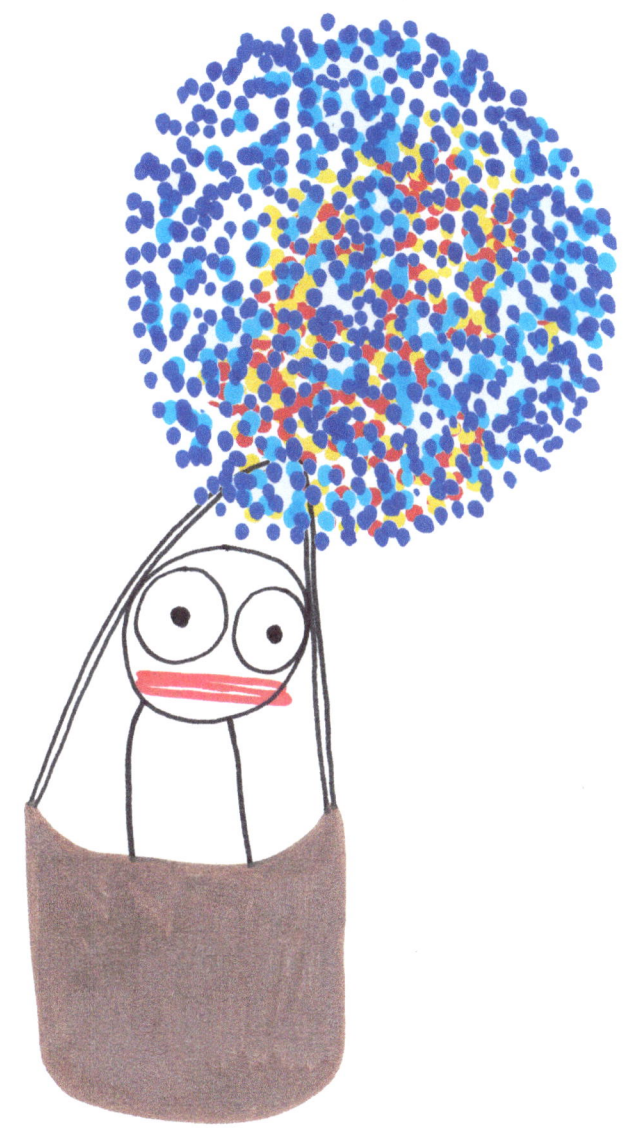

TAKE MORE RISKS.

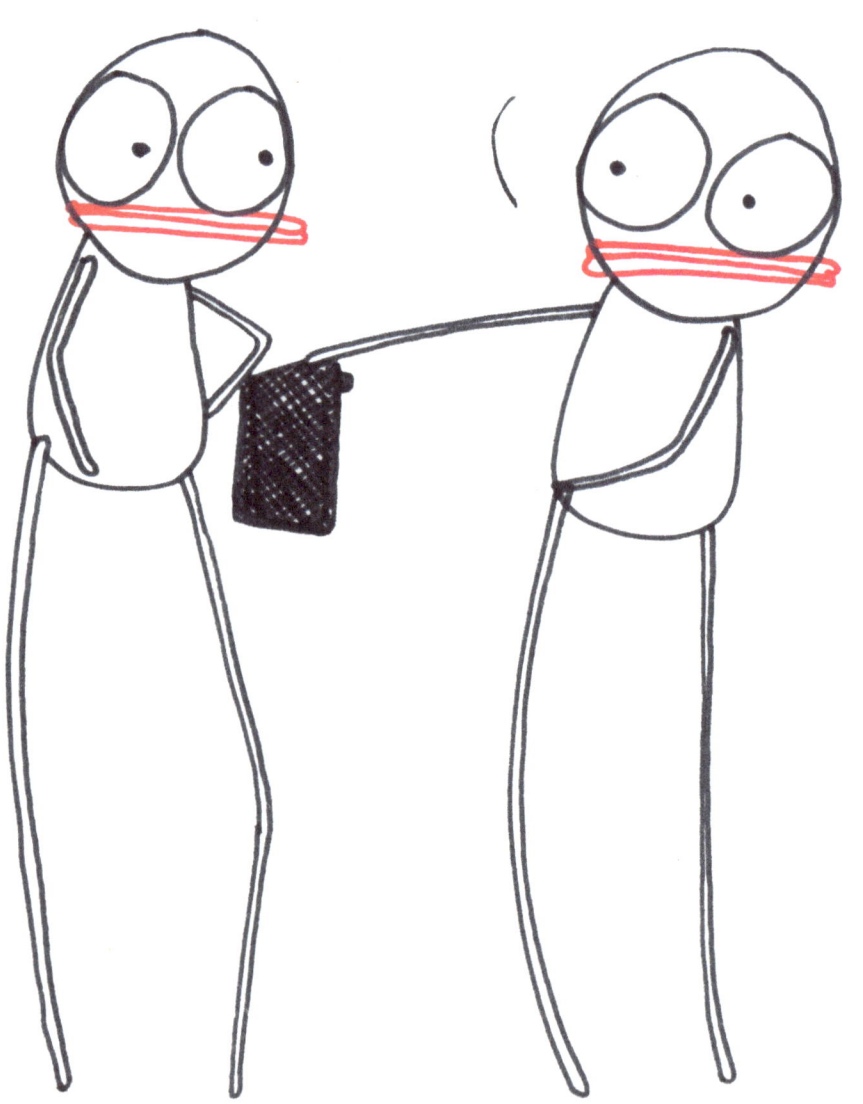

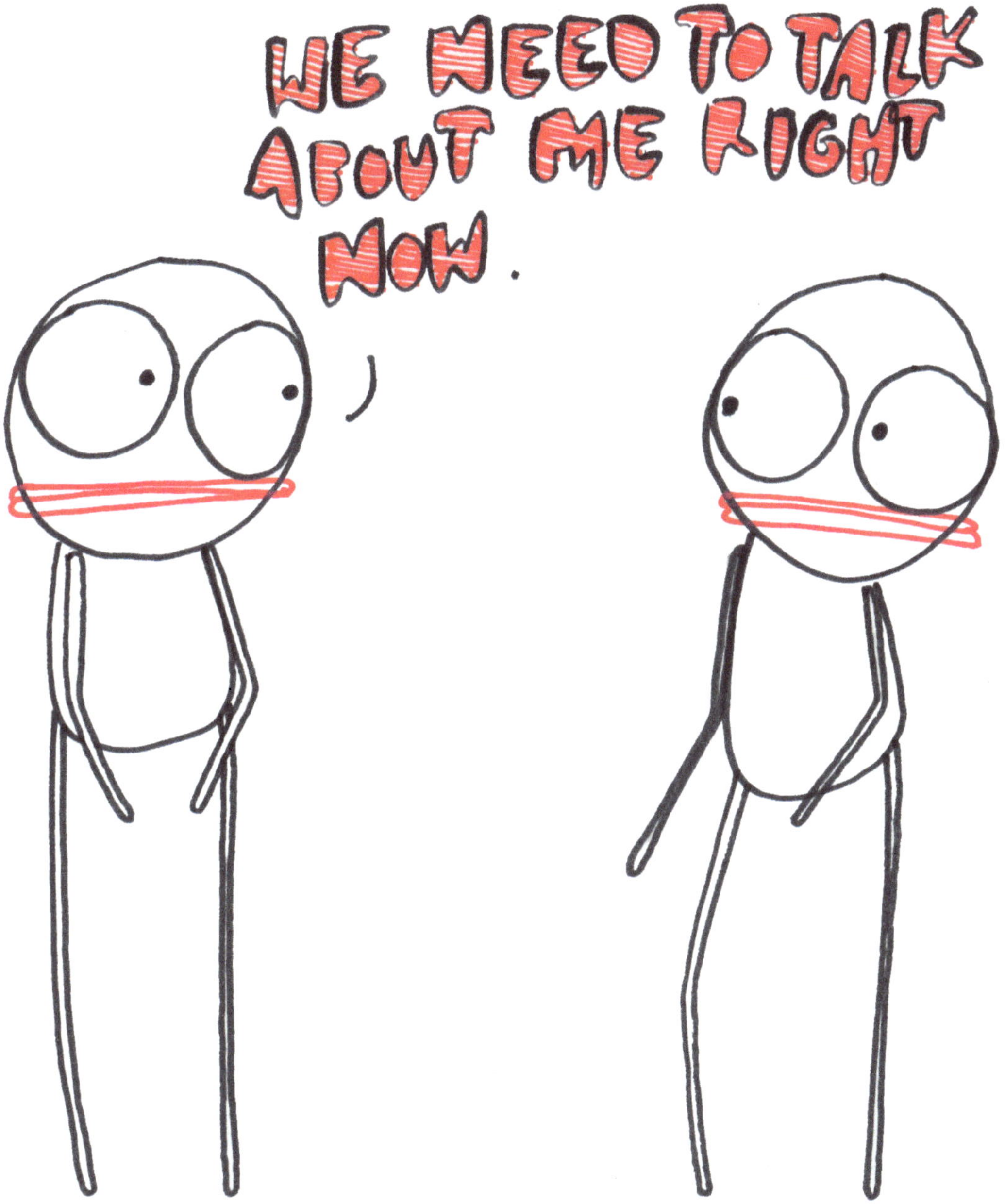

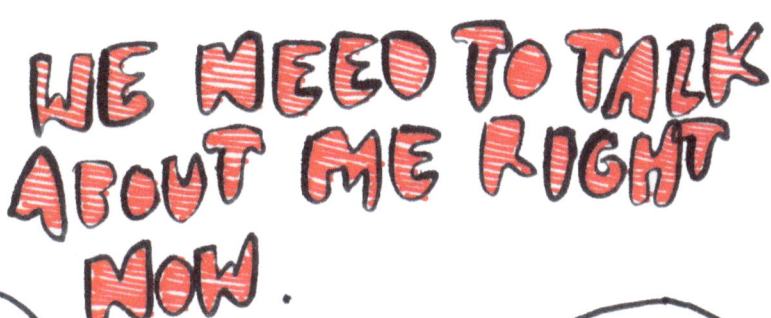

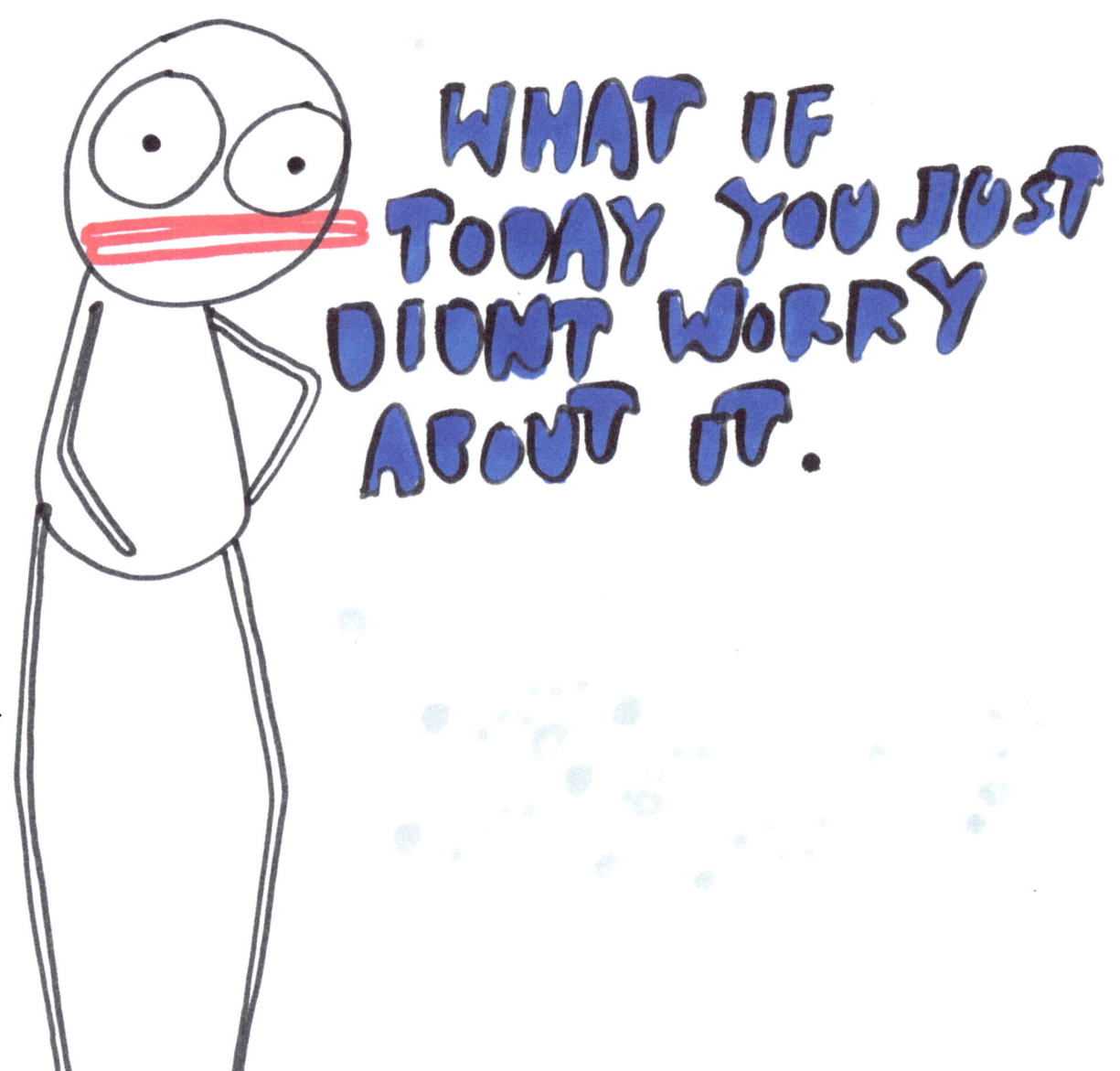

DON'T LET THE BASTARDS GET YOU DOWN.

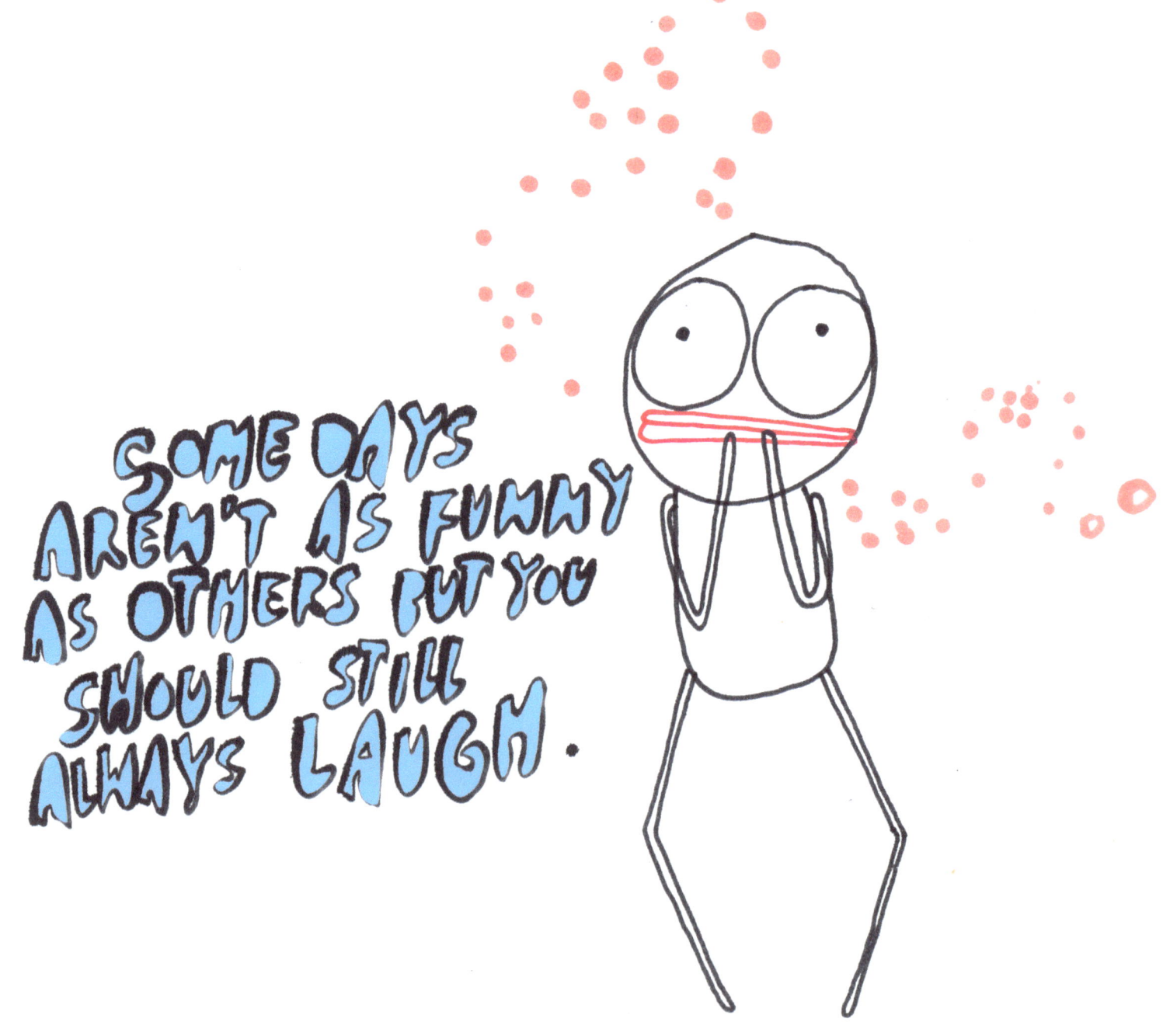

EVERYDAY I WISH IT WOULD STAY LIGHTER A LITTLE LONGER.

EVERYTHING IN MODERATION INCLUDING MODERATION.

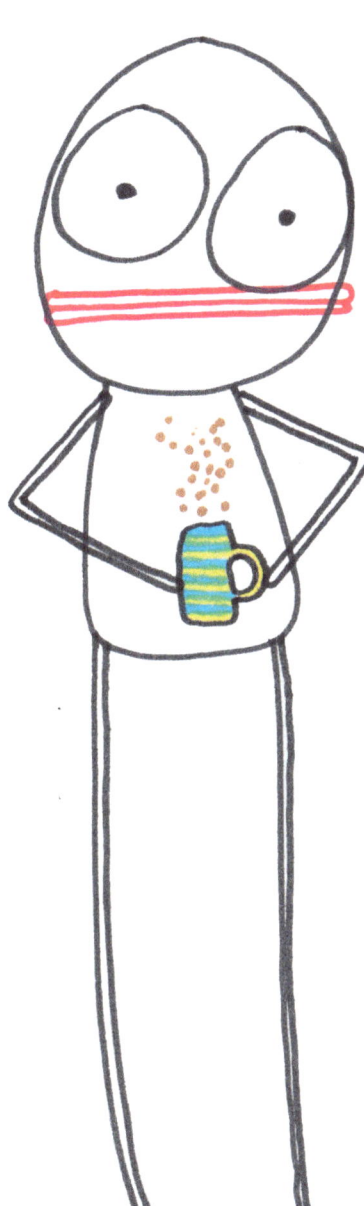

COFFEE
AND
BULLSHIT

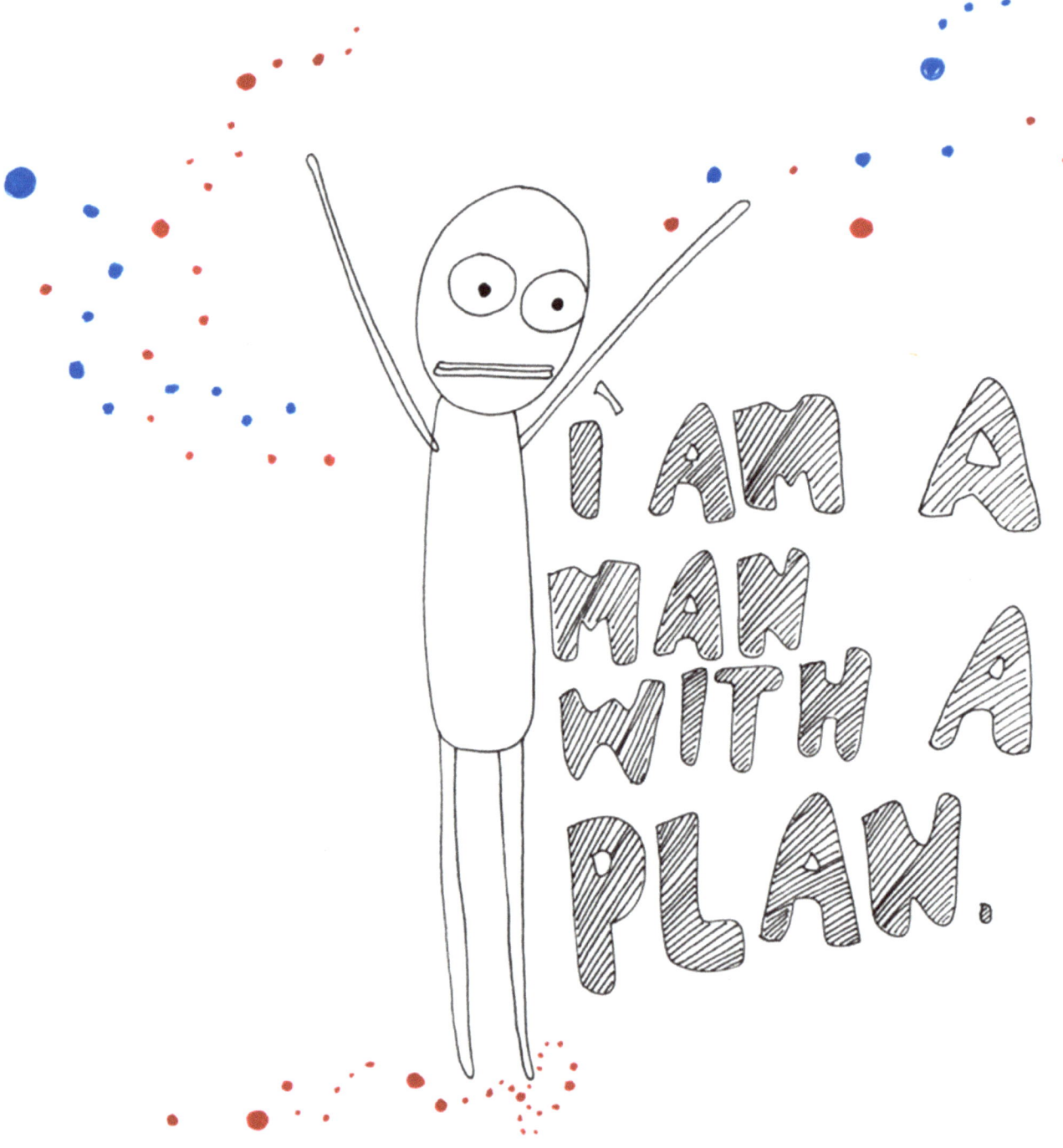

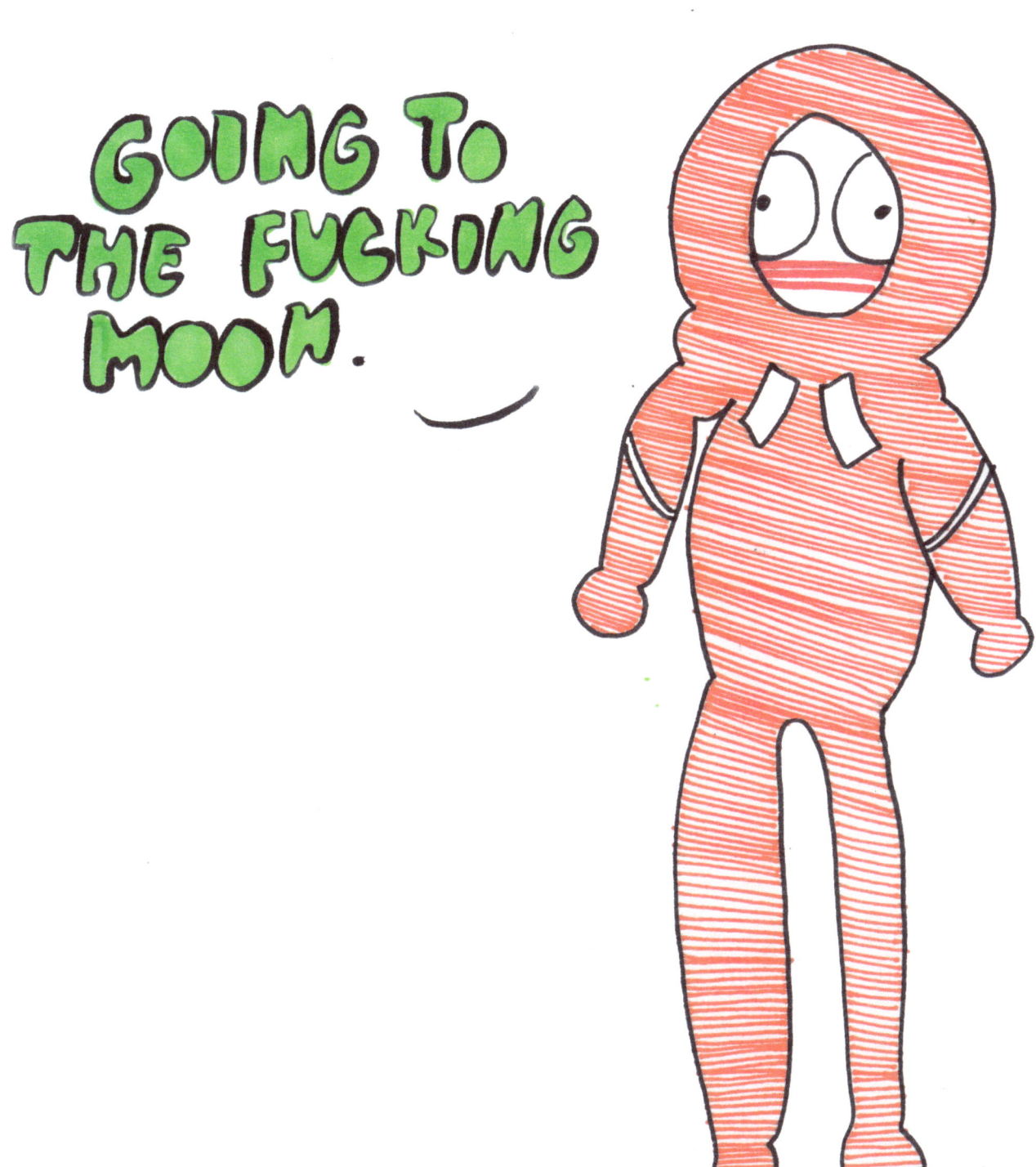

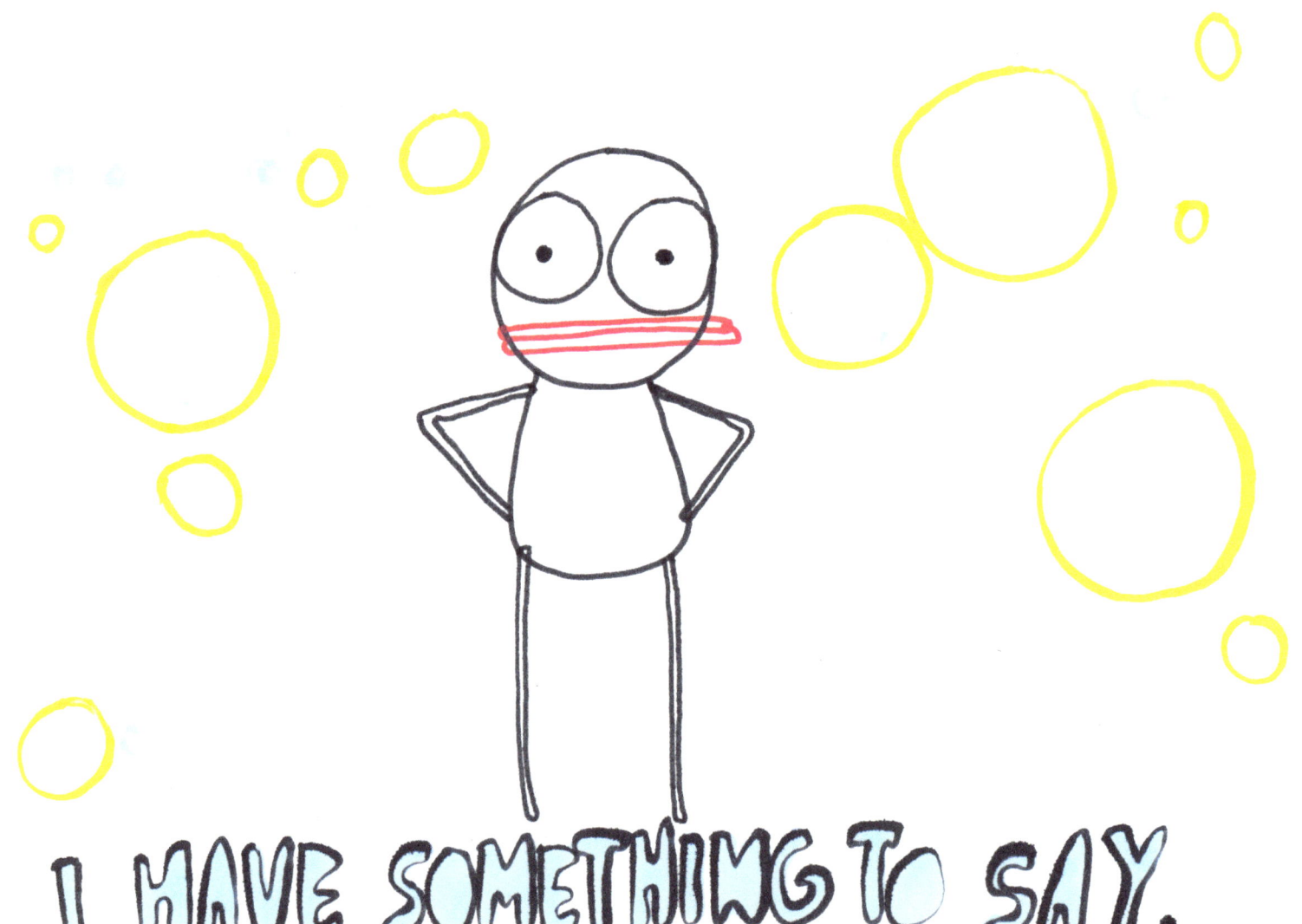

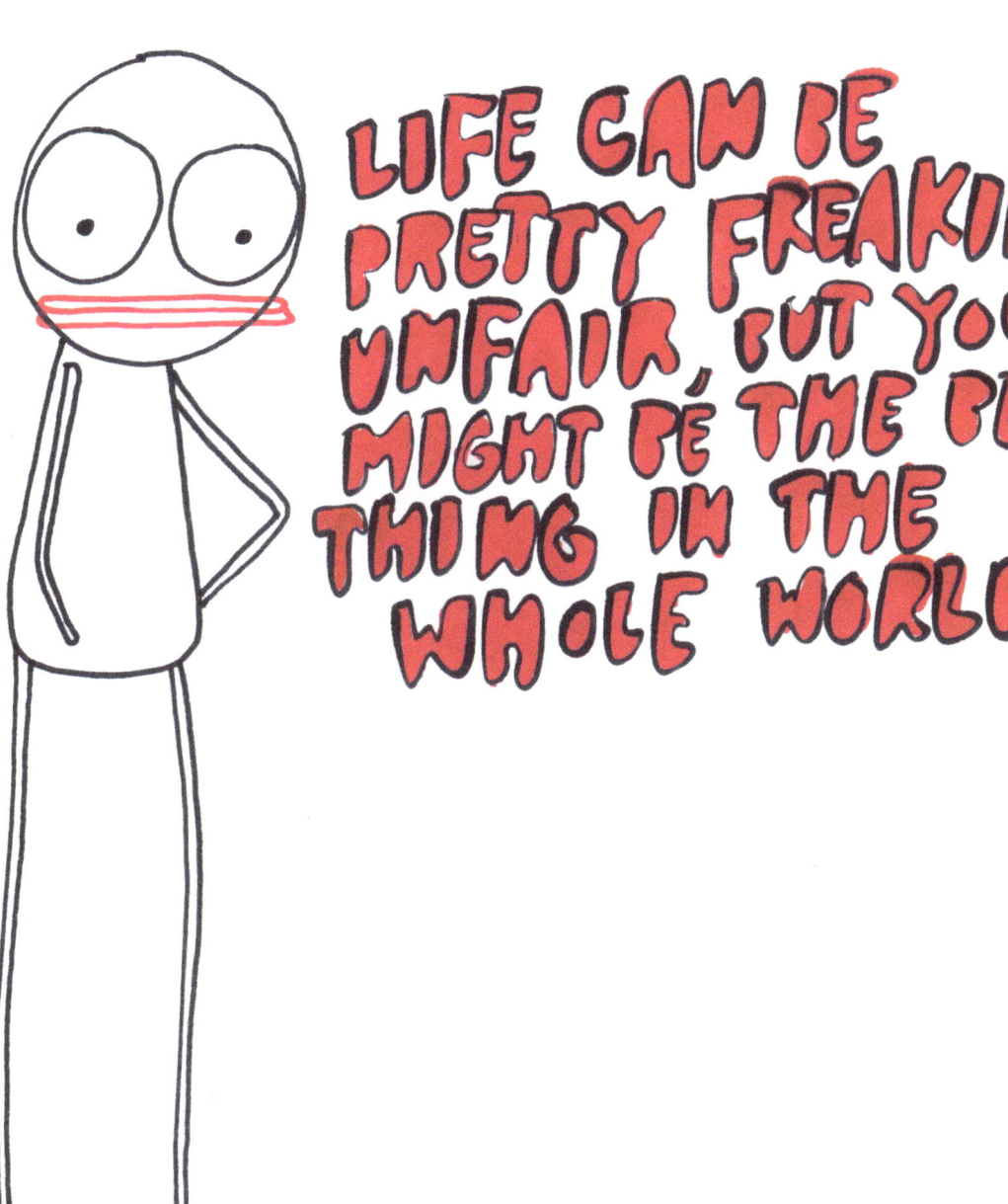

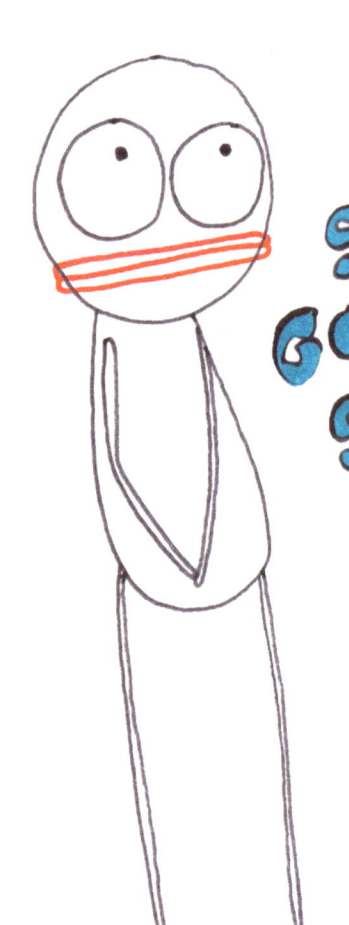

STARS UP THERE GOTTA MEAN SOMETHING.

THE TRUTH IS IN THE

SOMETIMES THINGS GO WRONG, BUT REALLY OFTEN THEY ALSO GO RIGHT.

IF I COULD I WOULD
KEEP THIS FEELING
IN A PLASTIC JAR.

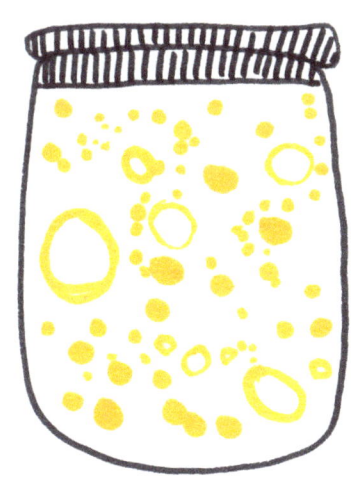

And they all lived happily ever after ...

THE END.

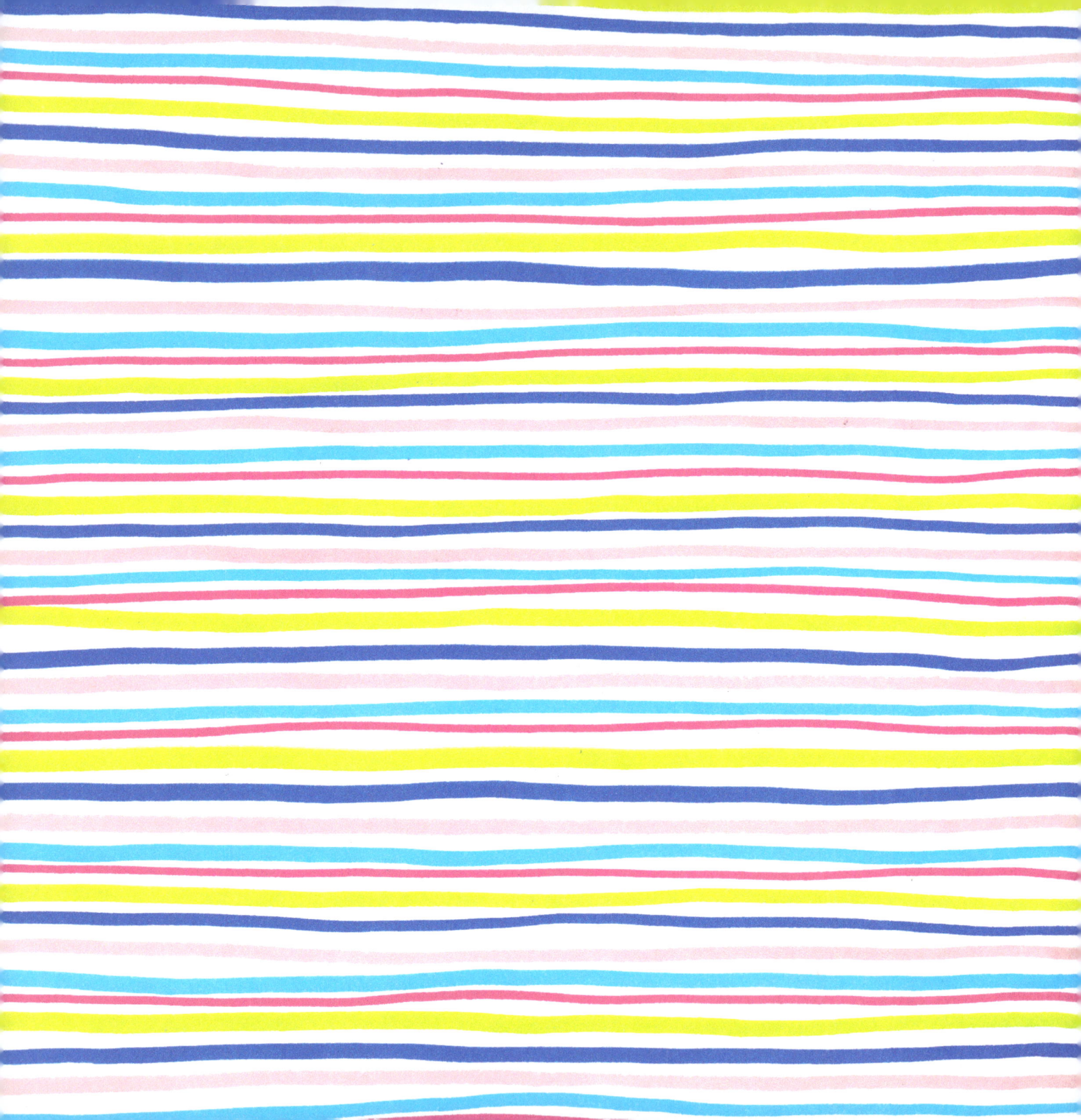

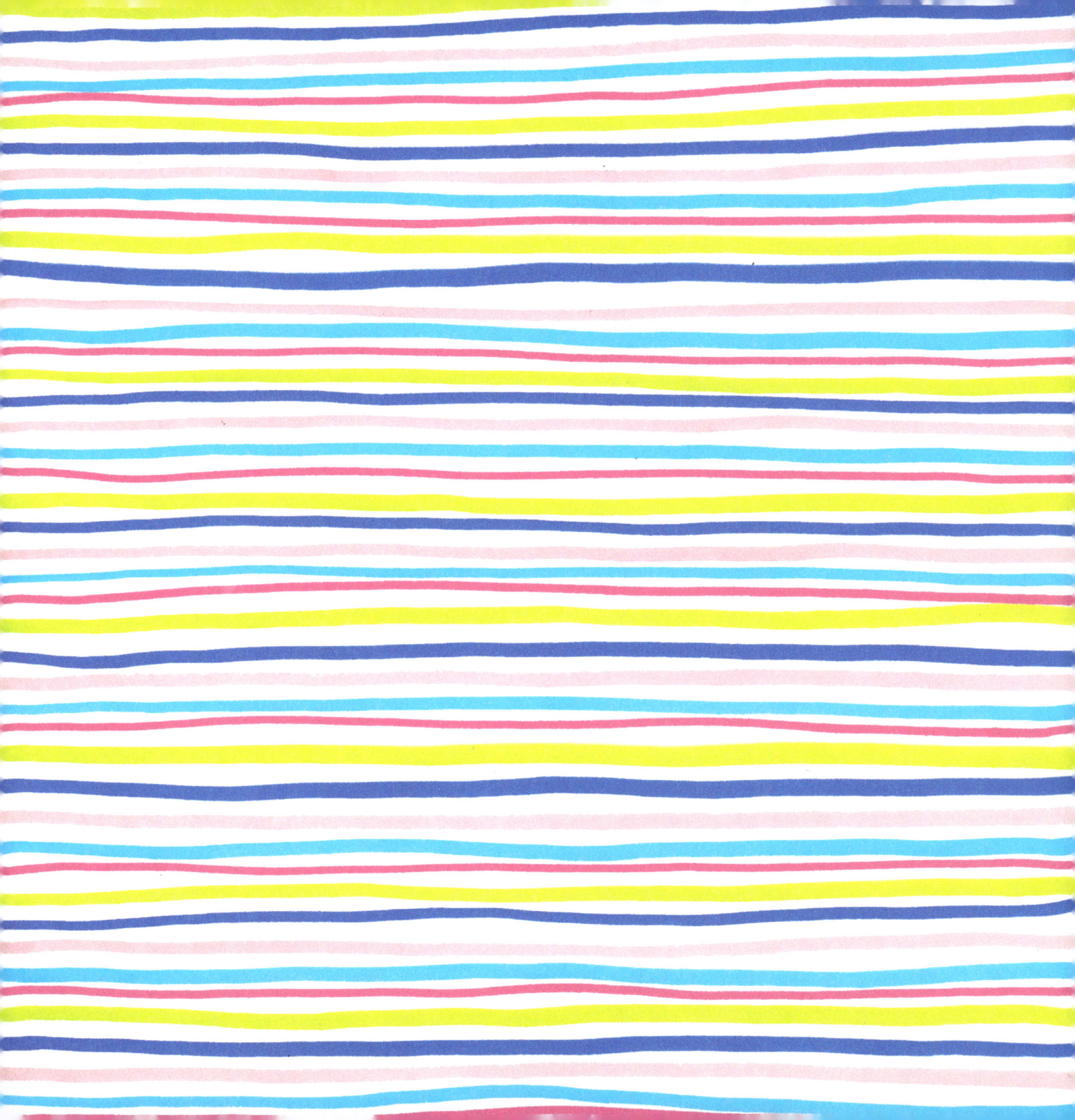